Revised & Updated John Williams Anthology

CONTENTS

Title	Source	Page
THEME FROM THE ACCIDENTAL TOURIST	THE ACCIDENTAL TOURIST	160
AMERICA...THE DREAM GOES ON		15
A BIG BEAUTIFUL BALL	NOT WITH MY WIFE YOU DON'T!	4
CANTINA BAND	STAR WARS	36
CAN YOU READ MY MIND?	SUPERMAN	49
CELEBRATION FANFARE	150TH ANNIVERSARY OF THE CITY OF HOUSTON	101
THEME FROM CLOSE ENCOUNTERS OF THE THIRD KIND	CLOSE ENCOUNTERS OF THE THIRD KIND	65
THEME FROM THE COWBOYS	THE COWBOYS	120
THE EMPEROR	RETURN OF THE JEDI	57
THEME FROM E.T. (THE EXTRA-TERRESTRIAL)	E.T. (THE EXTRA-TERRESTRIAL)	60
EXSULTATE JUSTI	EMPIRE OF THE SUN	136
EWOK CELEBRATION	RETURN OF THE JEDI	96
THE FOREST BATTLE	RETURN OF THE JEDI	82
HAN SOLO AND THE PRINCESS	THE EMPIRE STRIKES BACK	46
HAN SOLO RETURNS (AT THE COURT OF JABBA THE HUTT)	RETURN OF THE JEDI	80
HOLD YOU	THE FURY	28
A HYMN TO NEW ENGLAND		122
IF WE WERE IN LOVE	YES, GIORGIO	70
THE IMPERIAL MARCH (DARTH VADER'S THEME)	THE EMPIRE STRIKES BACK	44
THEME FROM "JAWS"	JAWS	26
LAND OF THE GIANTS	LAND OF THE GIANTS	8
LIBERTY FANFARE AND THEME	100TH BIRTHDAY OF THE STATUE OF LIBERTY	128
LUKE AND LEIA	RETURN OF THE JEDI	52
MAY THE FORCE BE WITH YOU	THE EMPIRE STRIKES BACK	126
THE MISSION THEME	NBC NEWS	112
NICE TO BE AROUND	CINDERELLA LIBERTY	12
OLYMPIC FANFARE AND THEME	1984 OLYMPIC GAMES	90
THE OLYMPIC GAMES	1988 OLYMPIC GAMES	170
PARADE OF THE EWOKS	RETURN OF THE JEDI	106
PRINCESS LEIA'S THEME	STAR WARS	74
RAIDERS MARCH	RAIDERS OF THE LOST ARK	76
REMEMBERING CAROLYN	PRESUMED INNOCENT	166
SOMEWHERE IN MY MEMORY	HOME ALONE	163
STAR WARS (MAIN THEME)	STAR WARS TRILOGY	24
THEME FROM "SUPERMAN"	SUPERMAN	32
TOYPLANES, HOME AND HEARTH	EMPIRE OF THE SUN	148
WINTER GAMES FANFARE	1989 WORLD ALPINE SKI CHAMPIONSHIP	153
YODA'S THEME	THE EMPIRE STRIKES BACK	41

© 1991 WARNER BROS. PUBLICATIONS INC.
All Rights Reserved

John Williams

AWARDS & NOMINATIONS

- ACADEMY AWARD NOMINATION .... HOME ALONE
  Best Score (1990)
- ACADEMY AWARD NOMINATION .... SOMEWHERE IN MY MEMORY
  Best Song (1990) (from HOME ALONE)
  (Composed music)
- ACADEMY AWARD NOMINATION .... INDIANA JONES AND THE LAST CRUSADE
  Best Score (1989)
- GRAMMY NOMINATION (1989) .... INDIANA JONES AND THE LAST CRUSADE
  Best Album of Orig. Instr. Background Score
- ACADEMY AWARD NOMINATION .... BORN ON THE FOURTH OF JULY
  (Best Score)
- GOLDEN GLOBE NOMINATION .... BORN ON THE FOURTH OF JULY
- ACADEMY AWARD NOMINATION .... ACCIDENTAL TOURIST
- GOLDEN GLOBE NOMINATION .... ACCIDENTAL TOURIST
- ACADEMY AWARD NOMINATION .... THE WITCHES OF EASTWICK
- GRAMMY NOMINATION (1987) .... THE WITCHES OF EASTWICK
  Best Album of Orig. Instr. Background Score
- BRITISH ACADEMY AWARD .... EMPIRE OF THE SUN
- GRAMMY NOMINATION (1988) .... EMPIRE OF THE SUN
  Best Album of Orig. Instrumental
- GRAMMY NOMINATION (1988) .... OLYMPIC SPIRIT
  Best Instr. Composition
- ACADEMY AWARD NOMINATION .... EMPIRE OF THE SUN
- ACADEMY AWARD NOMINATION .... THE RIVER
- ACADEMY AWARD NOMINATION .... INDIANA JONES: THE TEMPLE OF DOOM
  Best Orig. Score (1984)
- GRAMMY AWARD (1984) .... OLYMPIC FANFARE & THEME
  Best Instr. Composition
- ACADEMY AWARD NOMINATION .... RETURN OF THE JEDI
- GRAMMY NOMINATION (1983) .... RETURN OF THE JEDI
  Best Album of Orig. Score
- ACADEMY AWARD NOMINATION .... YES, GIORGIO "If We Were In Love"
  Best Original Score
- ACADEMY AWARD .... E.T.
- GRAMMY AWARD (1982) .... E.T.
  Best Album of Orig. Score
- GRAMMY AWARD (1982) .... FLYING (Theme from E.T.)
  Best Arrangement in instr. recording
- GRAMMY AWARD (1982) .... FLYING (Theme from E.T.)
  Best Instr. Composition
- GRAMMY NOMINATION (1982) .... E.T.
  Best Pop Instr. Perf.
- GRAMMY NOMINATION (1982) .... ADVENTURE ON EARTH
  Best Instr. Composition
- ACADEMY AWARD NOMINATION .... RAIDERS OF THE LOST ARK
- GRAMMY AWARD (1981) .... RAIDERS OF THE LOST ARK
  Best Album of Orig. Score
- ACADEMY AWARD NOMINATION .... THE EMPIRE STRIKES BACK
- GRAMMY AWARD (1980) .... THE EMPIRE STRIKES BACK
  Best Album of Orig. Score
- GRAMMY AWARD (1980) .... THE EMPIRE STRIKES BACK
  Best Instr. Composition
- GRAMMY NOMINATION (1980) .... YODA'S THEME
  Best Instr. Composition
- GRAMMY NOMINATION (1980) .... IMPERIAL MARCH (Darth Vader's Theme)
  Best Instr. Composition
- GRAMMY NOMINATION (1980) .... YODA'S THEME
  Best Pop Instr. Perf.
- GRAMMY AWARD (1979) .... SUPERMAN
  Best Album of Orig. Score
- GRAMMY AWARD (1979) .... SUPERMAN (Theme)
  Best Instr. Composition
- GRAMMY NOMINATION (1979) .... SUPERMAN (Theme)
  Best Pop Instr. Perf.
- ACADEMY AWARD NOMINATION .... SUPERMAN
- ACADEMY AWARD NOMINATION .... CLOSE ENCOUNTERS OF THE THIRD KIND
- GRAMMY AWARD (1978) .... CLOSE ENCOUNTERS OF THE THIRD KIND (Theme)
  Best Instr. Composition
- GRAMMY AWARD (1978) .... CLOSE ENCOUNTERS OF THE THIRD KIND
  Best Album of Orig. Score
- GRAMMY NOMINATION (1978) .... CLOSE ENCOUNTERS OF THE THIRD KIND
  Best Pop Instr. Perf.
- ACADEMY AWARD .... STAR WARS
- GRAMMY AWARD (1977) .... STAR WARS
  Best Pop Instr. Recording
- GRAMMY AWARD (1977) .... STAR WARS (Main Title)
  Best Instr. Composition
- GRAMMY AWARD (1977) .... STAR WARS
  Best Original Score for Motion Picture
- GRAMMY NOMINATION (1977) .... STAR WARS
  Album of the Year
- ACADEMY AWARD NOMINATION .... IMAGES
- ACADEMY AWARD .... JAWS
- GRAMMY AWARD (1975) .... JAWS
  Best Original Score Album
- ACADEMY AWARD NOMINATION .... THE TOWERING INFERNO
- ACADEMY AWARD NOMINATION .... CINDERELLA LIBERTY
  (song) Nice To Be Around
- ACADEMY AWARD NOMINATION .... CINDERELLA LIBERTY
  (score)
- ACADEMY AWARD NOMINATION .... THE POSEIDON ADVENTURE
- ACADEMY AWARD NOMINATION .... TOM SAWYER
- ACADEMY AWARD NOMINATION .... THE REIVERS
- ACADEMY AWARD .... FIDDLER ON THE ROOF
- ACADEMY AWARD NOMINATION .... GOODBYE MR. CHIPS
- ACADEMY AWARD NOMINATION .... VALLEY OF THE DOLLS
- GRAMMY NOMINATION .... CHECKMATE
  Best Soundtrack

MOTION PICTURES

- HOOK .... Tri-Star
  Frank Marshall/Kathy Kennedy
  Jerry Molen, prods.
  Steven Spielberg, dir.
- HOME ALONE .... Fox
  John Hughes, prod.
  Chris Columbus, dir.
- JFK .... Warner Brothers
  Arnon Milchan, ex. prod.
  H. Kittman Ho. prod.
  Oliver Stone, prod./dir.
- HOME ALONE .... Fox
  John Hughes, prod.
  Chris Columbus, dir.
- PRESUMED INNOCENT .... Warner Bros.
  Sydney Pollack/Mark Rosenberg, prods.
  Alan Pakula, dir.
- ALWAYS .... Universal/Amblin
  Frank Marshall/Kathleen Kennedy, prods.
  Steven Spielberg, dir.
- BORN ON THE 4TH OF JULY .... Universal
  Oliver Stone/A. Kitman Ho, prods.
  Oliver Stone, dir.
- STANLEY & IRIS .... MGM
  Alex Winitsky/Arlene Sellers, prods.
  Martin Ritt, dir.
- INDIANA JONES AND THE LAST CRUSADE ..... Paramount/Lucasfilm, Ltd.
  Robert Watts, prod.
  Steven Spielberg, dir.
- ACCIDENTAL TOURIST .... Warner Bros.
  Lawrence Kasdan/Charles Okun/
  Michael Grills, prods.
  Lawrence Kasdan, dir.
- RAIDERS OF THE LOST ARK .... Paramount
  George Lucas, prod.
  Steven Spielberg, dir.
- 1941 .... Universal/Columbia
  Steven Spielberg, dir.
- THE EMPIRE STRIKES BACK .... Fox
  George Lucas, prod.
  Irwin Kershner, dir.
- DRACULA .... Universal
  John Badham, dir.
- JAWS 2 .... Universal
  Jeannot Szwarc, dir.
- SUPERMAN .... Warner Bros.
  The Salkind Bros., prod.
  Richard Donner, dir.
- FURY .... Fox
  Frank Yablans, prod.
  Brian Di Palma, dir.
- CLOSE ENCOUNTERS OF THE THIRD KIND ..... Columbia
  Steven Spielberg, dir.
- STAR WARS .... Fox
  Gary Kurtz, prod.
  George Lucas, dir.
- BLACK SUNDAY .... Universal
- FAMILY PLOT .... Universal
  Alfred Hitchcock
- MIDWAY .... Universal
- THE MISSOURI BREAKS .... United Artists
  Jack Nicholson

- THE SUGARLAND EXPRESS .... Universal
  Steven Spielberg, dir.
- THE EIGER SANCTION .... Universal
- EARTHQUAKE .... Universal
  Irwin Allen, dir.
- IMAGES .... United Artists
  Robert Altman, dir.
- JAWS .... Universal
  Zanuck/Brown, prod.
  Steven Spielberg, dir.
- THE TOWERING INFERNO .... Warner Bros./Fox
  Irwin Allen, prod.
  John Guillermin, dir.
- THE PAPER CHASE .... Fox
  James Bridges, dir.
  Roderick Paul/Robert Thompson, prod.
- CINDERELLA LIBERTY .... Fox
  "Nice To Be Around"
  Mark Rydell, prod., dir.
- THE LONG GOODBYE .... Robert Altman, dir.
- THE POSEIDON ADVENTURE .... Fox
  Irwin Allen, prod.
  Ronald Neame, dir.
- PETE & TILLIE .... Universal
  Martin Ritt, dir.
- TOM SAWYER .... Fox
  Arthur Jacobson, prod.
  Don Taylor, dir.
- THE REIVERS .... Cinema Center Films
- FIDDLER ON THE ROOF .... The Mirisch Corporation,
  Norman Jewison, dir.
- GOODBYE MR. CHIPS .... MGM
  Herb Ross, dir.
  Arthur P. Jacobs, prod.
- GARDEN OF CUCUMBERS .... The Mirisch Corporation
- VALLEY OF THE DOLLS .... Fox
  Mark Robson, dir.
  David Weisbart, prod.
- A GUIDE FOR THE MARRIED MAN .... Fox
  Frank Mc Carthy, prod.
  Gene Kelly, dir.
- BACHELOR FLAT .... Fox
  Jack Cummings, prod.
  Frank Tashlin, dir.
- JOHN GOLDFARB, PLEASE COME HOME ..... Fox
  Steve Parker, prod.
  J. Lee Thompson, dir.
- DIAMOND HEAD .... Columbia
  Jerry Bressler, prod.
- THE RARE BREED .... Universal
- NONE BUT THE BRAVE .... Warner Bros.
  Howard W. Koch, prod.
  Frank Sinatra, dir.
- PENELOPE .... MGM
  Arthur Loew Jr., prod.
  Arthur Hiller, dir.
- HOW TO STEAL A MILLION .... Fox
  Fred Kohlman, prod.
  William Wyler, prod./dir.

TELEVISION

- NBC NEWS THEME (1985) .... NBC
- AMAZING STORIES (theme) .... Amblin Entertainment/Universal
- 1988 SUMMER OLYMPICS THEME .... NBC

A BIG BEAUTIFUL BALL

Words by
JOHNNY MERCER

Music by
JOHN WILLIAMS

Jazz Waltz (Brightly)

Hey look-a me ma ma-ma I'm danc-in' _____ And I might som-er-sault right o-ver the wall. _____ This is-n't a {girl/beau} but a whole

© 1966 WARNER BROS. INC.
All Rights Reserved

world I'm ro-manc-in' And we're hav-in' A BIG BEAU-TI-FUL BALL. It's like I went and got high on a wee tod-dy, Yes sir-ree mate-y I feel eight-y feet tall. My heav-ens a-bove ev-'ry-one loves ev-'ry-bod-y And we're hav-in' A

G7 (sus. 4) C Am6 B7 B7+5
BIG BEAU - TI - FUL BALL. Fun - ny old world I just a -
E Ebm7 Ab7 Db
dore you, Fond - ly I im - plore you,
Dm7 G7 C A7 Dm7 Abo
You old trou - ba - dour, you, please, When you get read - y I'd
G7-5 G7 Go Dm7 Em Dm7 Cm7
like to go stead - y And gee, take it from me, it - 'll be groov - y

Cm7 F° Cm7
Cmaj.7
'Cause there's some-bod-y up there dig-gin' us all,
Cm7
Cmaj.7 C F6 (G bass) Em F (G bass) G
Dm7
Old chap-pie it ends hap-py just like in a mov-ie And we're hav-in' us
Dm7 G7 (sus. 4)
1.
C Em7
one fab-u-lous, fan-tab-u-lous, beau-ti-ful ball.
F G7
2.
C Dm7 C
ball.

LAND OF THE GIANTS

Music by
JOHN WILLIAMS

© 1969, 1970 WARNER-TAMERLANE PUBLISHING CORP.
All Rights Reserved

9

8va
Piano, W.W.
Cls.
Bssn.
Trpts.
Trpts.
Hrns.
Hrns.
Trbs., Organ
Piano
W.W.
W.W.
Cls.
Piano
W.W.
Fls.

11

NICE TO BE AROUND

(From the Twentieth Century-Fox Motion Picture "CINDERELLA LIBERTY")

Words by
PAUL WILLIAMS

Music by
JOHN WILLIAMS

"Hel - lo," such a sim - ple way to start a love af - fair: Should I jump right in and say how much I care? Would you take me for a mad man or a sim-ple-heart-ed clown?

"Hel - lo," with af - fec - tion from a sen-ti-men-tal fool to a lit - tle girl who's brok-en ev-'ry rule, one who brings me up when all the oth-ers seem to let me down.

know that the nic-est things have nev-er seemed to last, that we're both a bit em-bar-rassed by our past. But I think there's some-thing spe-cial in the feel-ings that we've found.

"Hel— To one who's nice to be a-

© 1973 WARNER-TAMERLANE PUBLISHING CORP. & ALMO MUSIC CORP.
All rights administered by WARNER-TAMERLANE PUBLISHING CORP.
All Rights Reserved

round, _____ should I say that "it's a blue world with-

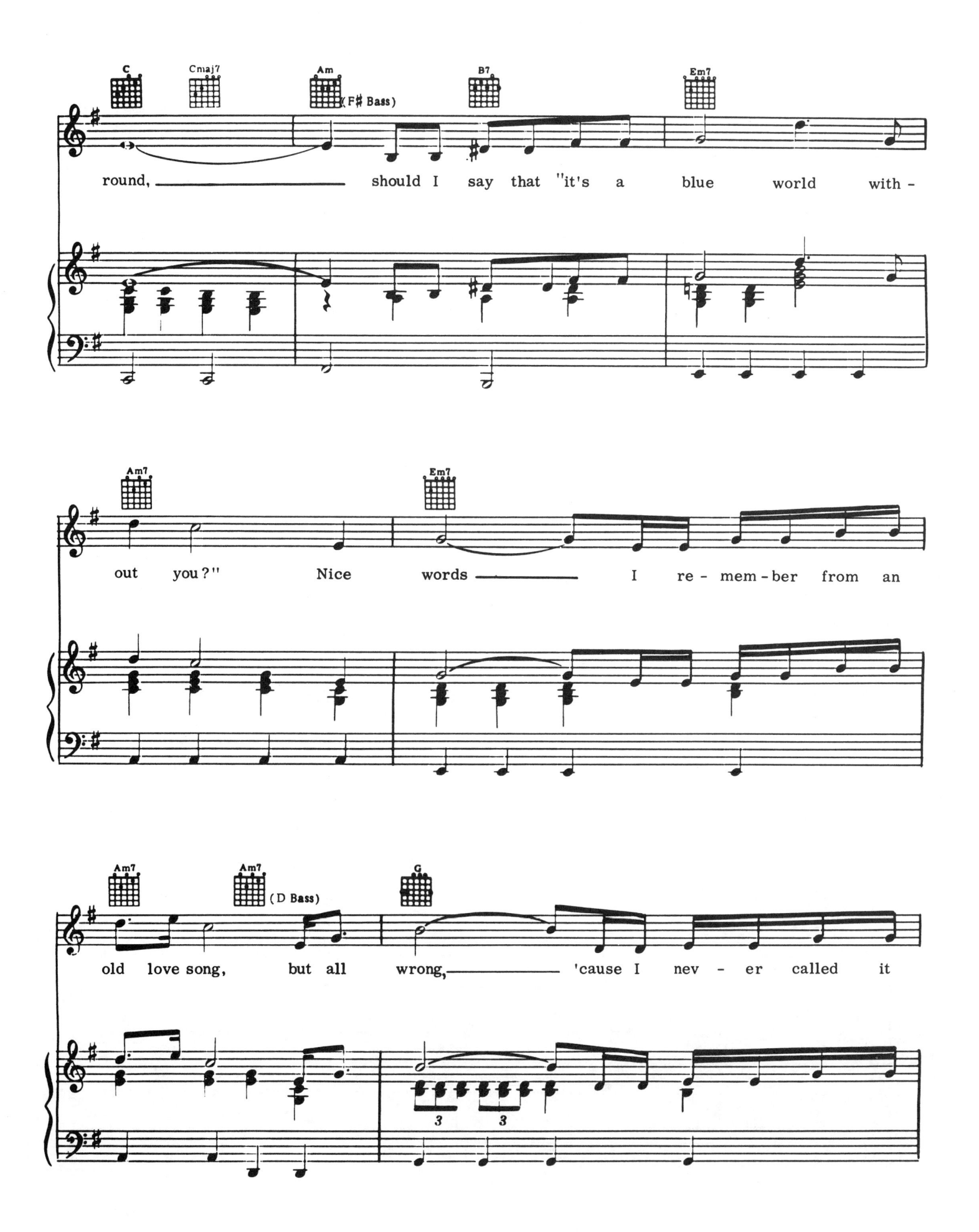

out you?" Nice words _____ I re-mem-ber from an

old love song, but all wrong, _____ 'cause I nev-er called it "love" be-fore. This feel-ing's new; this came with you. I _____ And you're nice to be a-round. And you're nice to be a-round. round.

rit.

AMERICA... THE DREAM GOES ON

Words by
ALAN & MARILYN BERGMAN

Music by
JOHN WILLIAMS

Majestically

GROUP: A-mer-i-ca, ___ A-mer-i-ca, ___ and the dream goes on! A-mer-i-ca, ___ A-mer-i-ca, ___ and the dream goes on! SOLOIST: There's a

© 1982, 1984 THREESOME MUSIC CO. (ASCAP)
All Rights Reserved

song in the dust of a coun-try road; on the wind it comes to call, ___ and it
words that we read on the court-house walls are the words that make us free, ___ and the

sings in the farms and the fac-t'ry towns and where you'd think there'd be no song at
more we re-mem-ber the way we be-gan, the clos-er we get to the best we can

all. And the words are the words that our fa-thers heard as they
be. Was there ev-er a time we for-got its worth, all the

whist-led down the years, and the name of the song is the name of the dream and it's
strug-gles and the scars, if we leave to the child-ren a sky full of hope and a

mu-sic to our ears. A - mer - i - ca, A -
flag that's filled with stars.

mer - i - ca, and the dream goes on! A -

-mer-i-ca, A-mer-i-ca, and the dream goes on! And the mer-i-ca, A-mer-i-ca, and the dream goes on! Re-member the voice of Jef-fer-son and the sound of Thom-as Paine, Lin-coln

sang at Gettysburg about America. Listen well to the wind and you can hear from Oregon to Maine, America, America! There's a song in the dust of a country road; it's a song we must recall, and it sings in the farms and the fac-t'ry towns, and where you'd think there'd be no song at all. And the words are the words that our fa-thers heard as they whis-tled down the years, and the name of the song is the name of the dream and it's music to our ears. A - mer - i - ca, A -

mer - i - ca, ___ and the dream goes on! ___

___ Think of Roos - e - velt and Ken - ne - dy ___ and of

Mar - tin Luth - er King, ___ and the way they sang ___ a song ___ a - bout A -

mer - i - ca. ___ Lis - ten well to the wind, it's al - ways there, ___ and it's

Fm
Db
4fr.
C
ask - ing us to sing: A - mer - i - ca, A - mer - i - ca!
ff
F
SOLOIST: Though the
f
F
Eb
voic - es are chang - ing, the song's the same as it sings from sea to sea, and as
F
Eb
long as the mu - sic is strong and clear, we'll know that to - mor - row will al - ways be

free. A-mer-i-ca, and the dream goes on! A-mer-i-ca, and the dream goes on! GROUP: A-mer-i-ca. A-mer-i-ca. A-mer-i-ca. A-mer-i-ca and the dream goes on!

STAR WARS
(Main Title)
From the Lucasfilm Ltd. Production - A Twentieth Century-Fox Release "STAR WARS"

Music by
JOHN WILLIAMS

March (Majestic)

© 1977 WARNER-TAMERLANE PUBLISHING CORP. & BANTHA MUSIC
All rights administered by WARNER-TAMERLANE PUBLISHING CORP.
All Rights Reserved

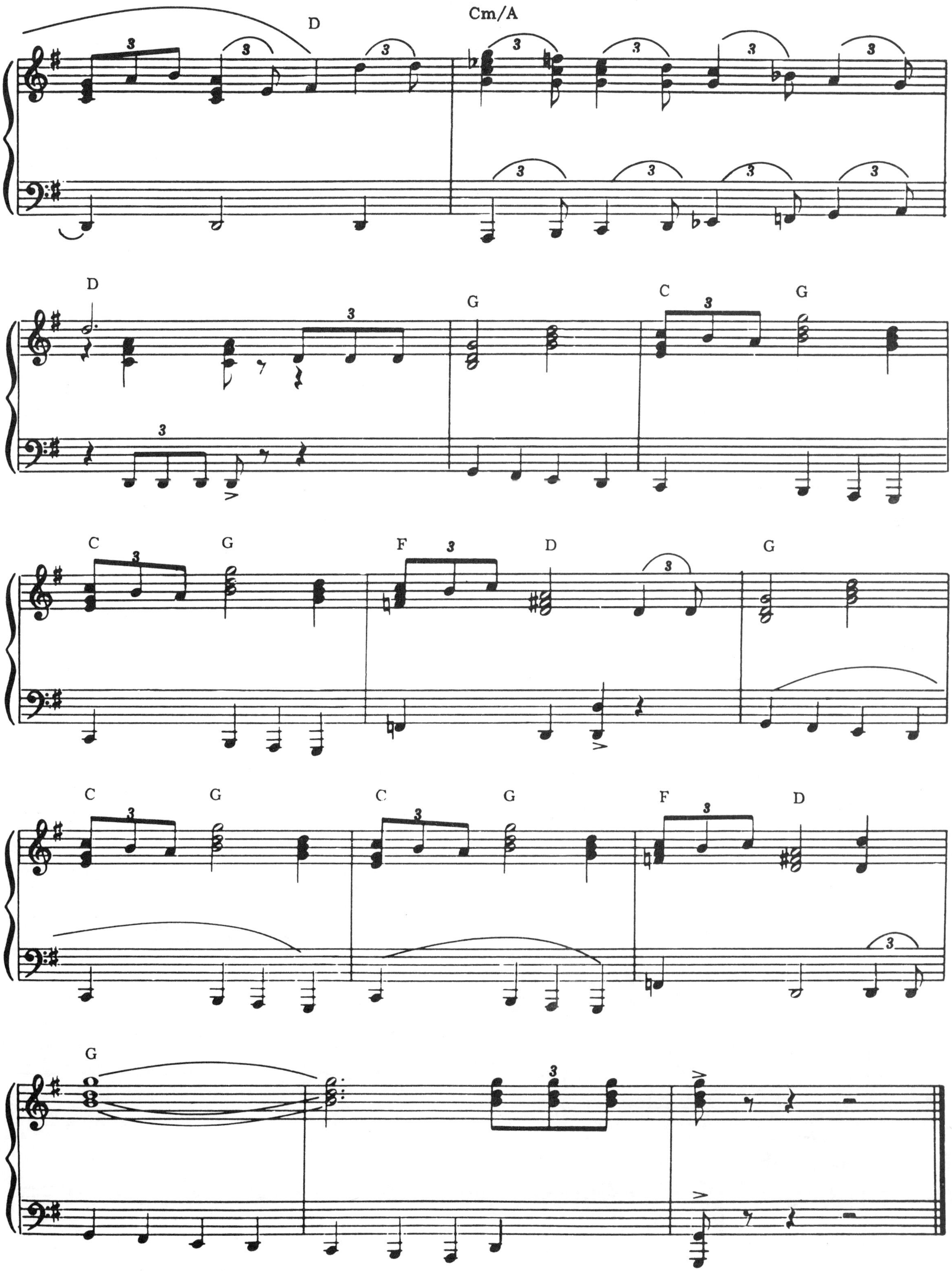
D
Cm/A
D
G
C
G
C
G
F
D
G
C
G
C
G
F
D
G

THEME FROM "JAWS"

By JOHN WILLIAMS

Very steady and threatening

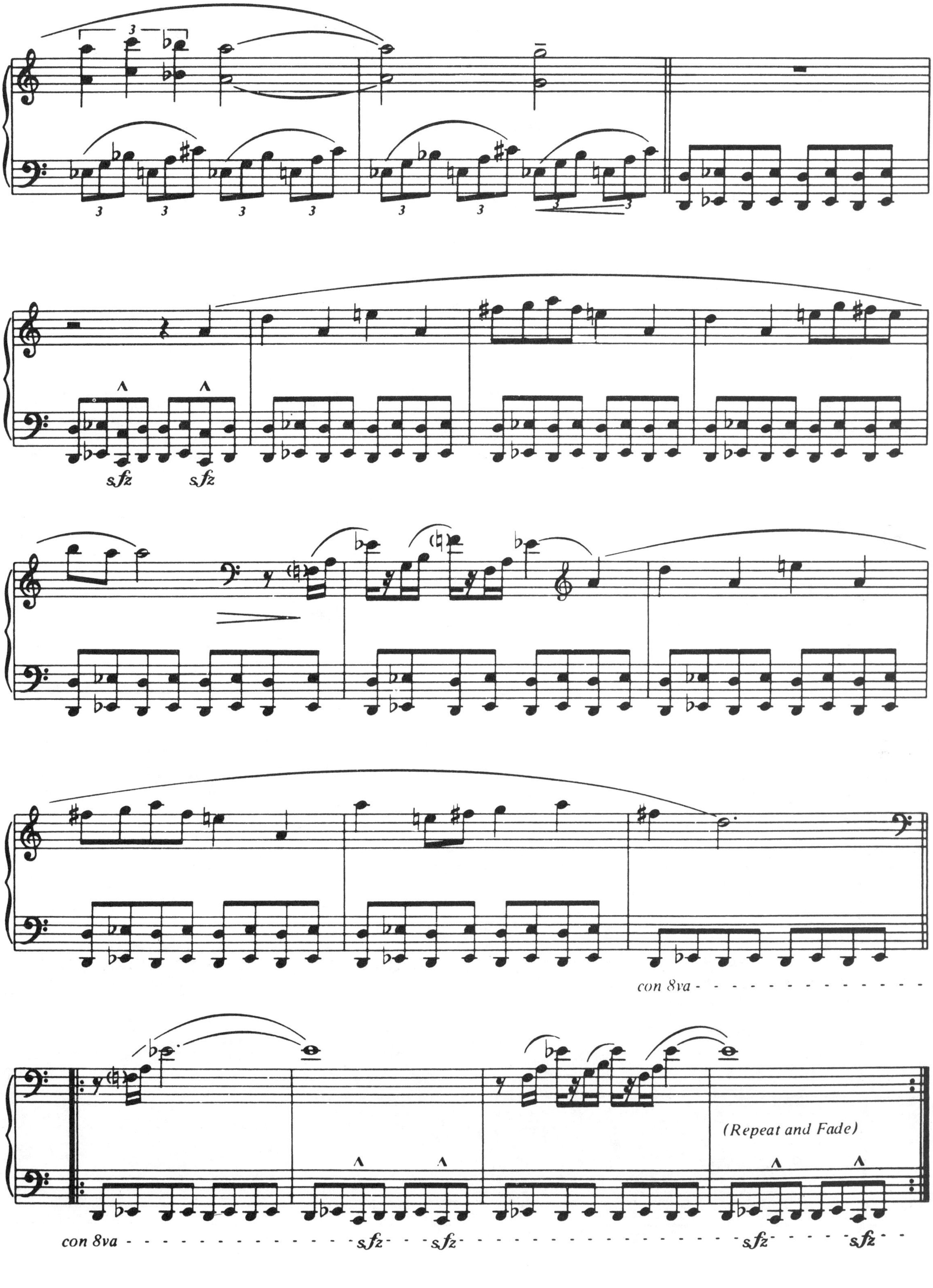
sfz
sfz
con 8va
con 8va
sfz
sfz
(Repeat and Fade)
sfz
sfz

HOLD YOU

Lyrics by
JOE WILLIAMS

Music by
JOHN WILLIAMS

Moderately ♩ = 92

1. Here I am so far from home and
2. Instrumental

all I wan-na do is hold you, yeah.

© 1978 WARNER-TAMERLANE PUBLISHING CORP.
All Rights Reserved

Yeah, _____ and I'm al-ways think-in' a-bout you ____ can't get you out-a my mind. ____ I wan-na feel you, I wan-na touch you, I wan-na be where you are, know that you're mine, nev-er be far ____ and love all the time, yeah. ____

When I left you, I never knew how long they'd keep me away from you, oh yeah. I'm always thinkin' about you, can't get you out-'a my mind. I wanna feel you, I wanna touch you, I wanna be where you are, know that you're mine, never be far

A E C D
— and love all the time, yeah. Yes, I love you, I love —
E
1. C D E
you. Yes, I love you, I love — you.
2. C D E
Repeat and fade
love you, I love — you. Yes, I
mf
f

THEME FROM "SUPERMAN"
A Warner Bros. Picture

By
JOHN WILLIAMS

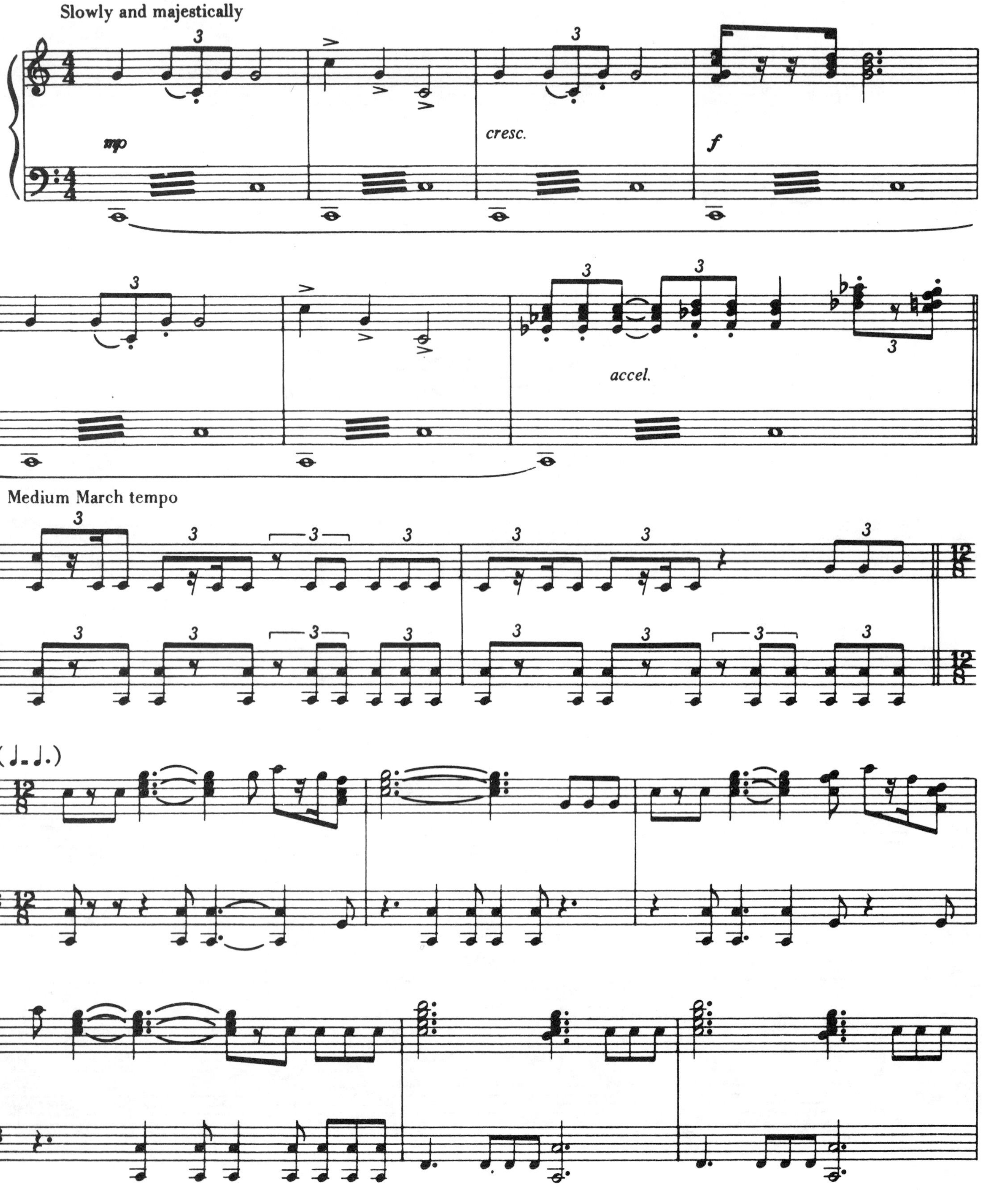

33

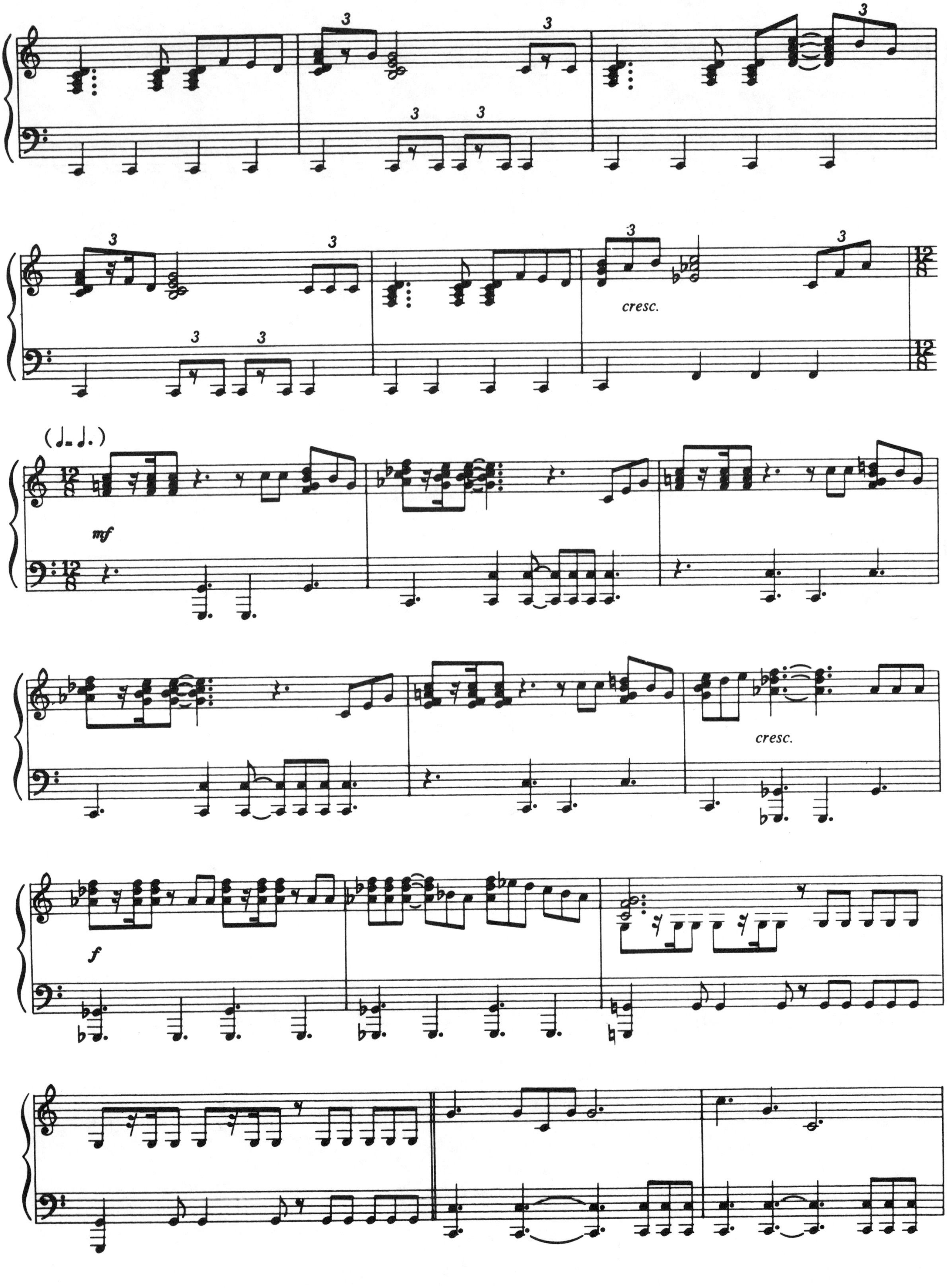
cresc.
mf
cresc.
f

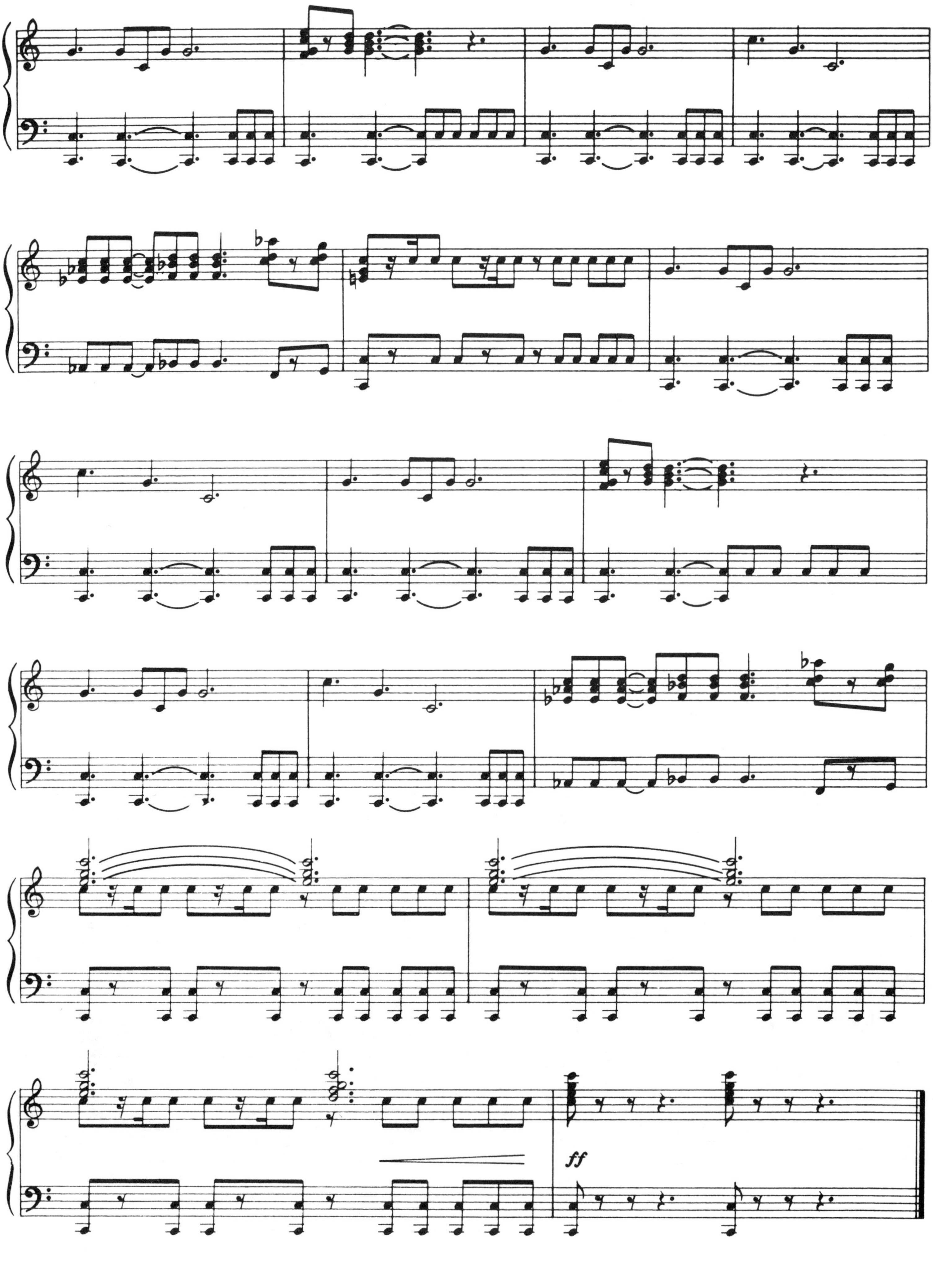
ff

CANTINA BAND

From the Lucasfilm Ltd. Production - A Twentieth Century-Fox Release "STAR WARS"

Music by
JOHN WILLIAMS

© 1977 WARNER-TAMERLANE PUBLISHING CORP. & BANTHA MUSIC
All rights administered by WARNER-TAMERLANE PUBLISHING CORP.
All Rights Reserved

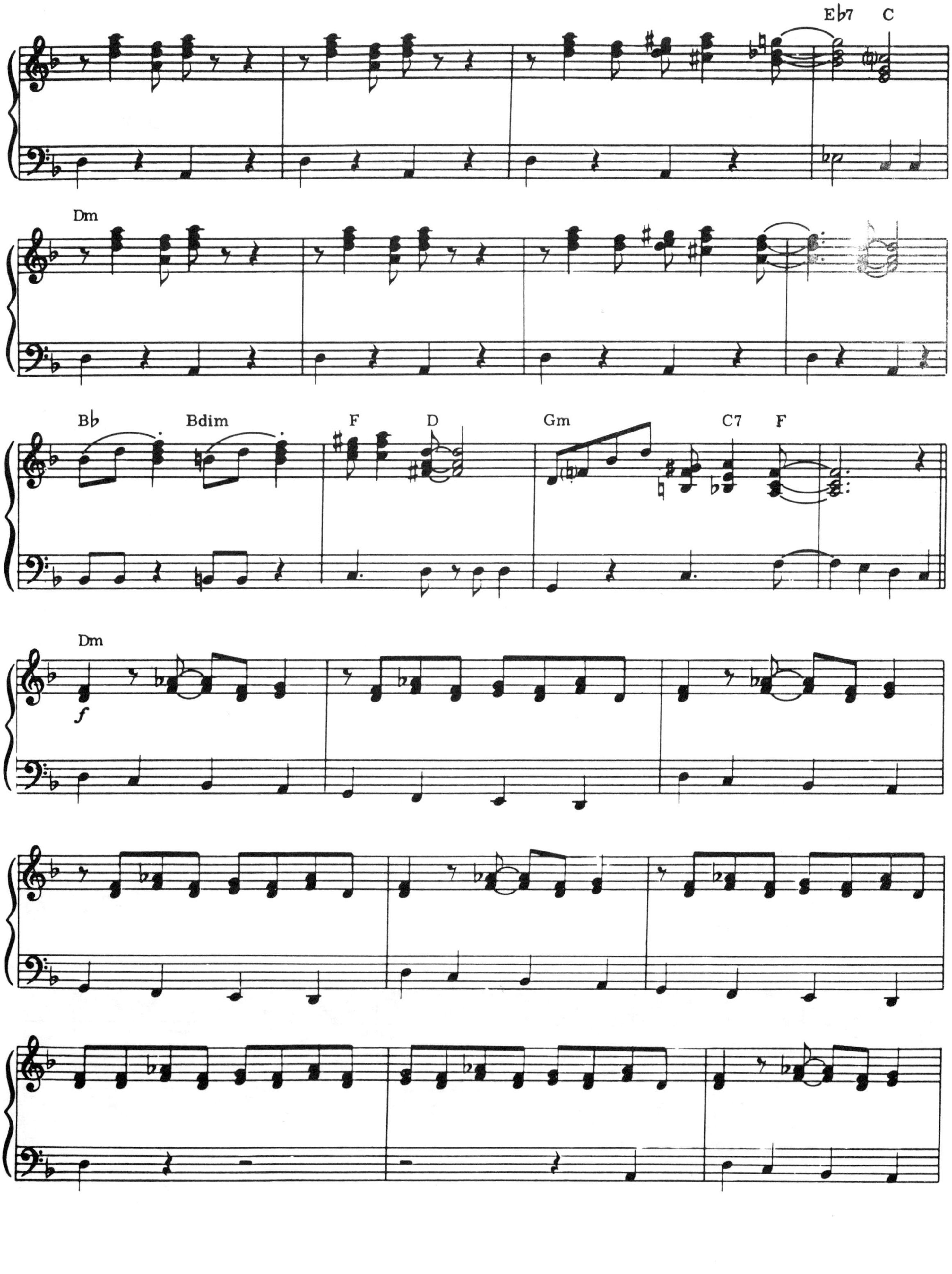
E♭7
C
Dm
B♭
Bdim
F
D
Gm
C7
F
Dm
f

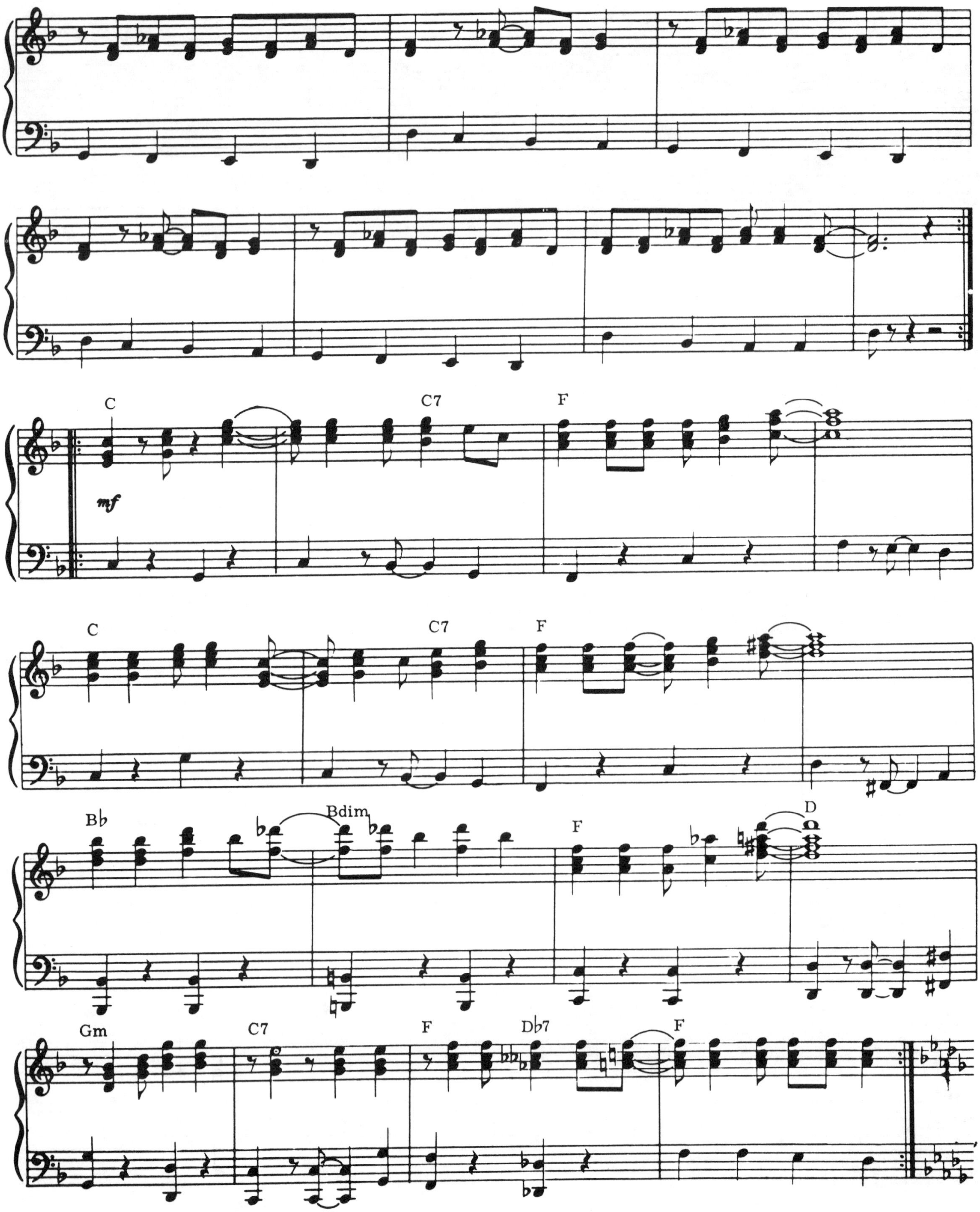
C
C7
F
mf
C
C7
F
B♭
Bdim
F
D
Gm
C7
F
D♭7
F

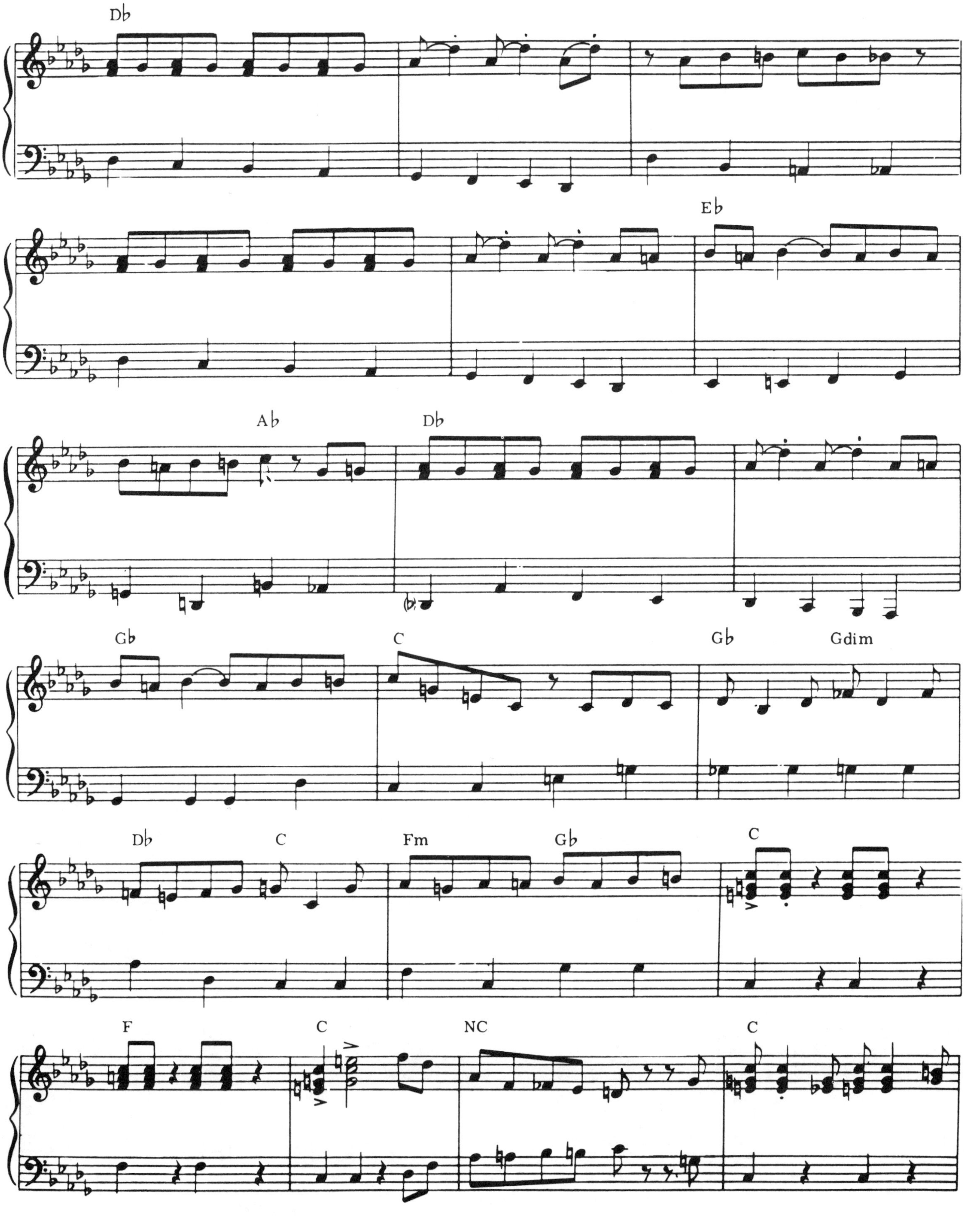
Db
Eb
Ab
Db
Gb
C
Gb
Gdim
Db
C
Fm
Gb
C
F
C
NC
C

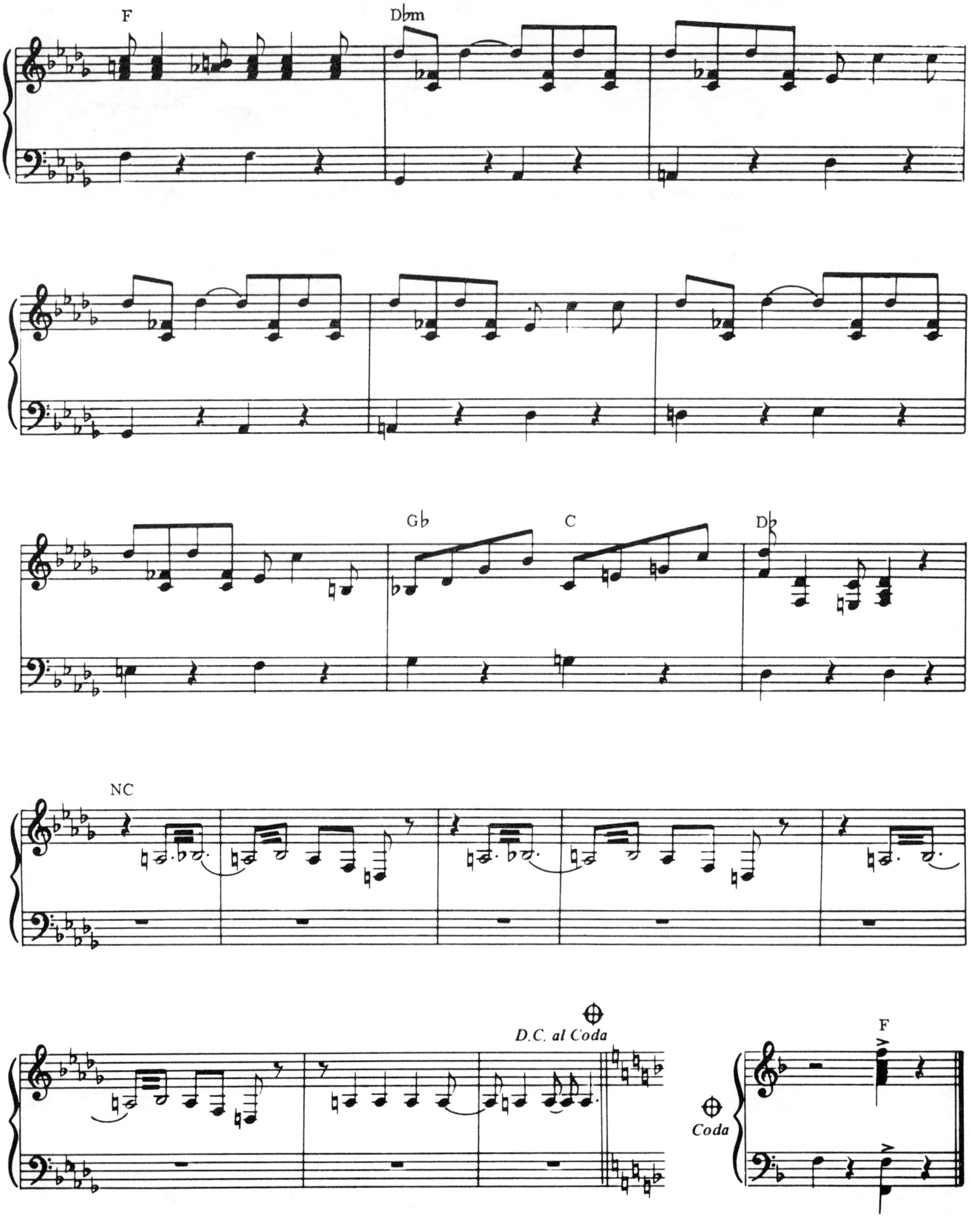
F
D♭m
G♭
C
D♭
NC
D.C. al Coda
Coda
F

YODA'S THEME

From "THE EMPIRE STRIKES BACK", A Lucasfilm Ltd. Production - A Twentieth Century-Fox Release

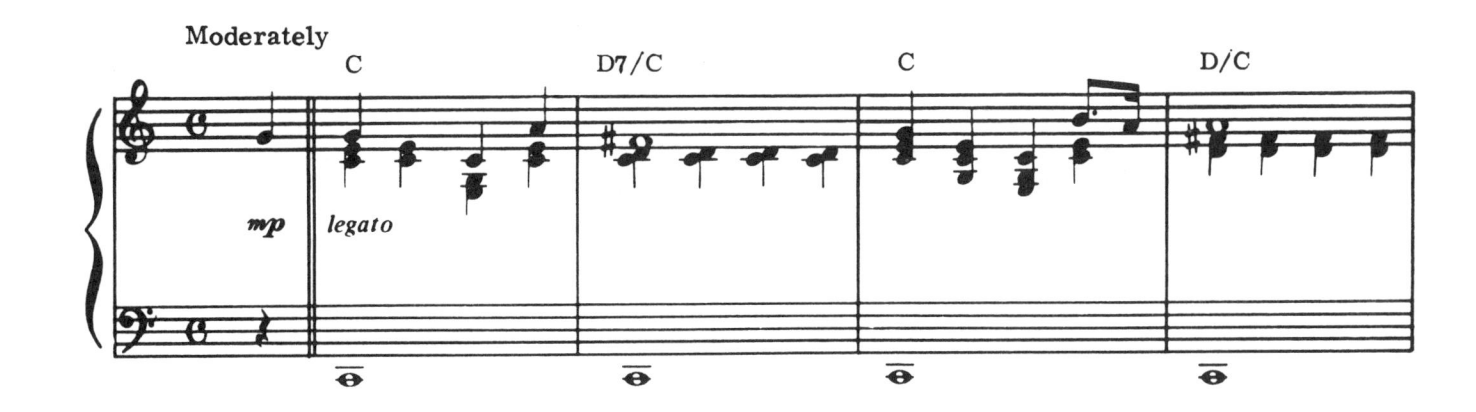

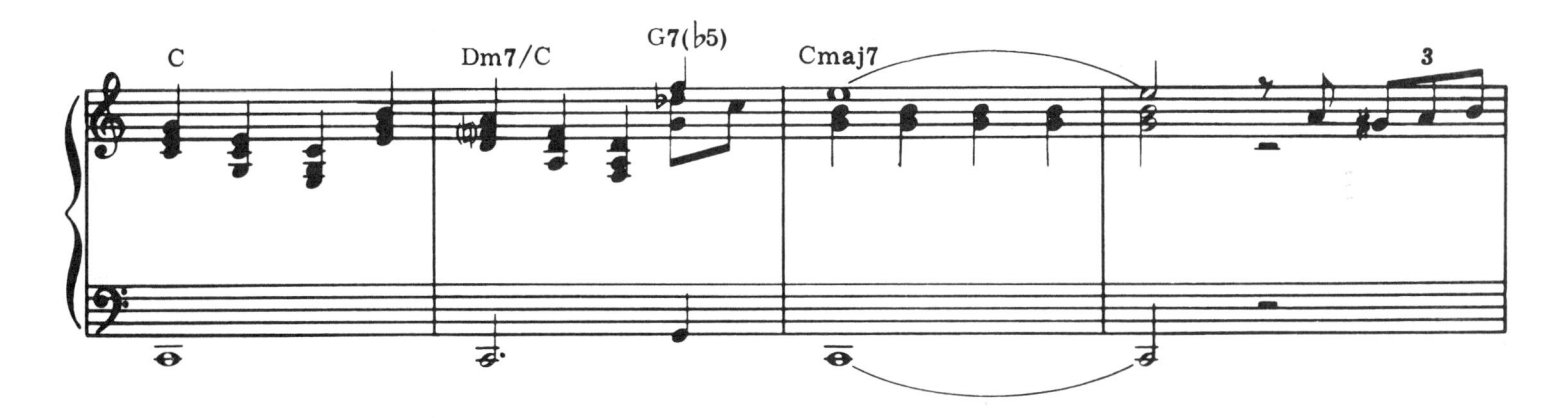

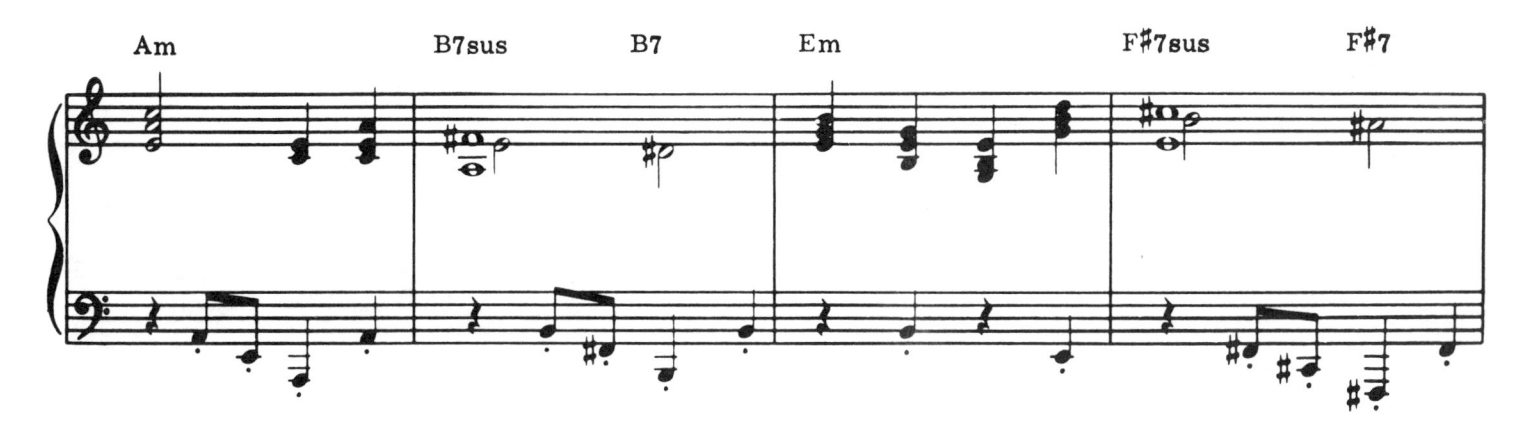

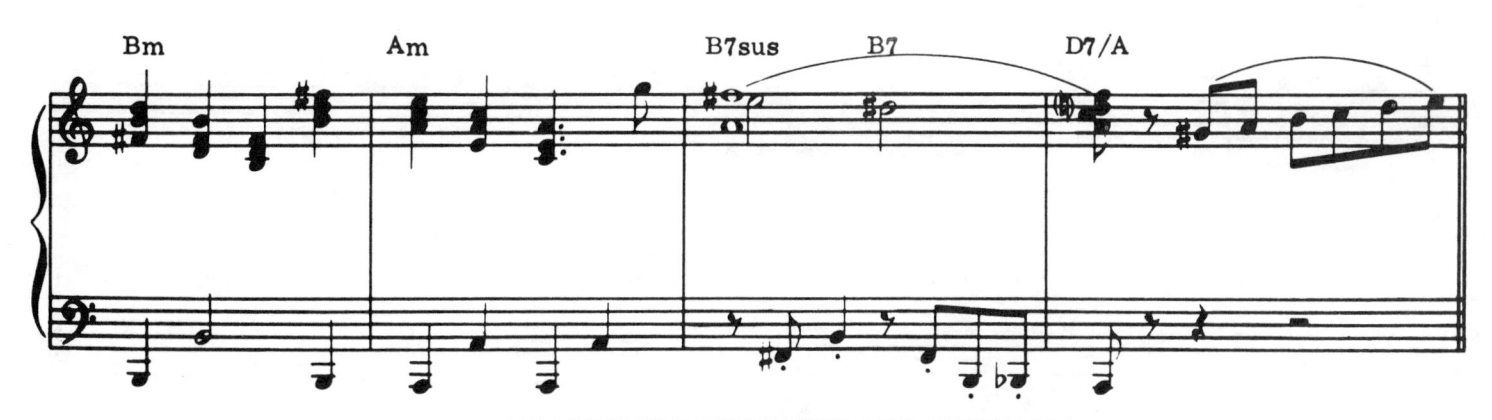

Music by
JOHN WILLIAMS

© 1980 WARNER-TAMERLANE PUBLISHING CORP. & BANTHA MUSIC
All rights administered by WARNER-TAMERLANE PUBLISHING CORP.
All Rights Reserved

A Little Faster
F
C/G
F/C
C
mf
F
C/G
F/G
C
Em/G
Bm
Em/B
Bm
F
F
D♭
B♭
A♭
G
poco rit.

C
D7/C
C
D/C
a tempo
Dm7
G7(♭5)
Cmaj7
Fm(♯7)/A♭
C
mp
p
D7/C
Em/B
B♭
B♭/A
Freely
Gm7
rit.
mp
Fm/G
C
p

THE IMPERIAL MARCH
(Darth Vader's Theme)
From "THE EMPIRE STRIKES BACK", A Lucasfilm Ltd. Production - A Twentieth Century-Fox Release

Music by
JOHN WILLIAMS

© 1980 WARNER-TAMERLANE PUBLISHING CORP. & BANTHA MUSIC
All rights administered by WARNER-TAMERLANE PUBLISHING CORP.
All Rights Reserved

45

HAN SOLO AND THE PRINCESS

(From "THE EMPIRE STRIKES BACK")

Music by
JOHN WILLIAMS

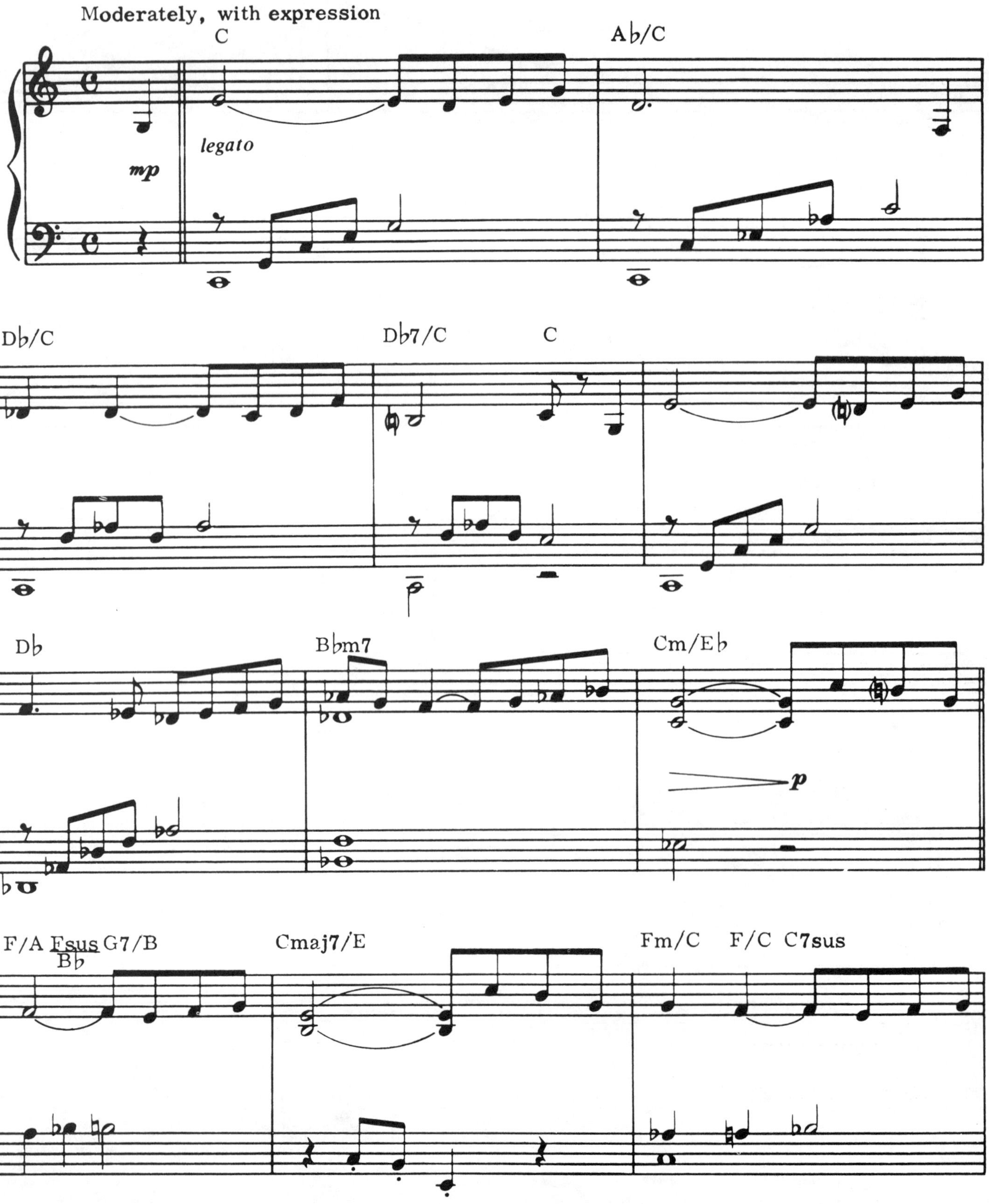

Cmaj7
Fm
Gb
mp
Ebm7
Gm7(b5)
G7(b5)
C
mf
rit.
a tempo
Ab/C
Db/C
Db7
C
To Coda
Db
Bbm7

B♭m7/A♭
Gm7(♭5)
G7(♭9)(♭5)
C
D.S. al Coda
rit.
Coda
D♭
B♭m7
accel. poco a poco
D♭/C
B♭m7
B♭m/A♭
Gm7(♭5)
G7(♭9)(♭5)
C
8va
f
ff
molto rit.
a tempo
mp
ff

Can You Read My Mind?
Love Theme From "SUPERMAN"

Lyric by
LESLIE BRICUSSE

Music by
JOHN WILLIAMS

© 1978 WARNER-TAMERLANE PUBLISHING CORP.
All Rights Reserved

hands___ with a god or a fool. Will you look at me quiv-er-ing like a lit-tle girl shiv-er-ing. You can see right through me. Can you read my mind? Can you pic-ture the things I'm think-ing of?___ Won-d'ring why you are all the won-der-ful things you

E♭7sus4 B♭7 B♭m7 E♭7sus4 A♭maj7
4 fr.
are. You can fly. You be-long to the sky. You and
B♭m7 E♭7sus4 Fm7-5 B♭7 E♭ F7/E♭
I could be-long to each oth - er. If you need a friend,
Fm7 Gm7 A♭ Fm7 B♭7sus4 B♭7 E♭ A♭maj7
3 fr.
4 fr.
4 fr.
I'm the one to fly to. If you need to be
E♭ A♭maj7 Am7-5 Cm/D G
4 fr.
4 fr.
3 fr.
loved, here I am. Read my mind!

LUKE AND LEIA

From the Lucasfilm Ltd. Production - A Twentieth Century-Fox Release "RETURN OF THE JEDI"

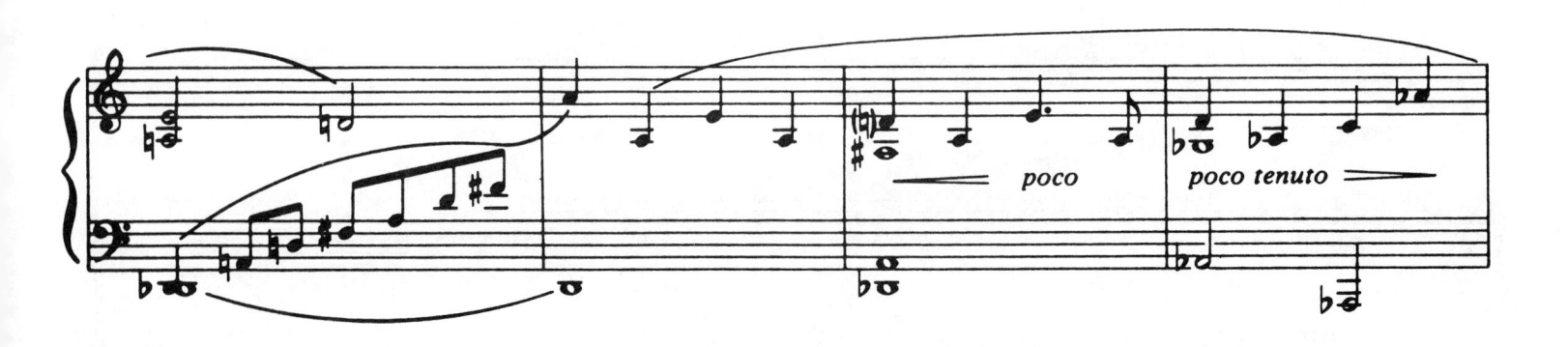

Music by
JOHN WILLIAMS

© 1983 BANTHA MUSIC
All rights administered by WARNER-TAMERLANE PUBLISHING CORP.
All Rights Reserved

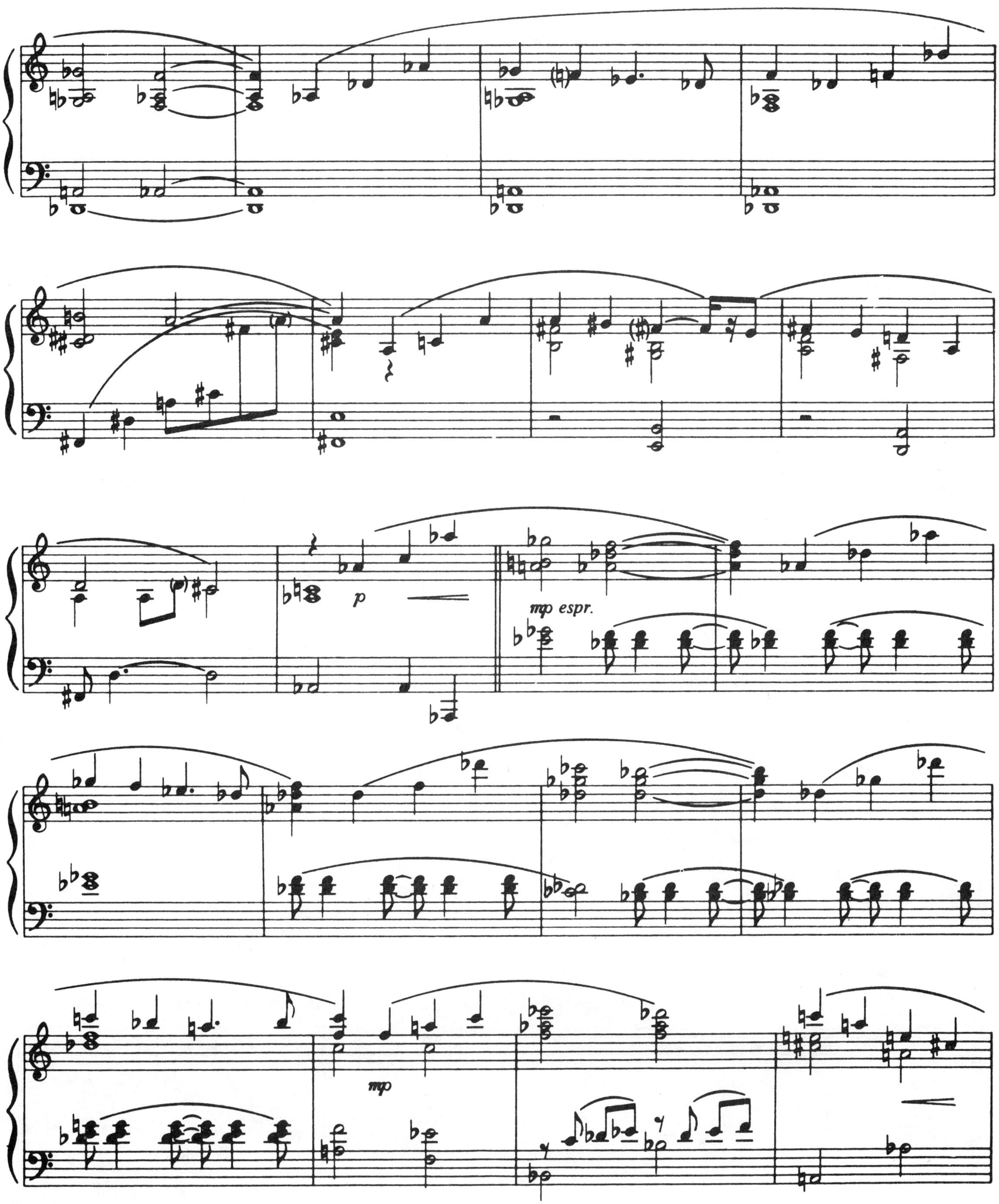
p
mp espr.
mp

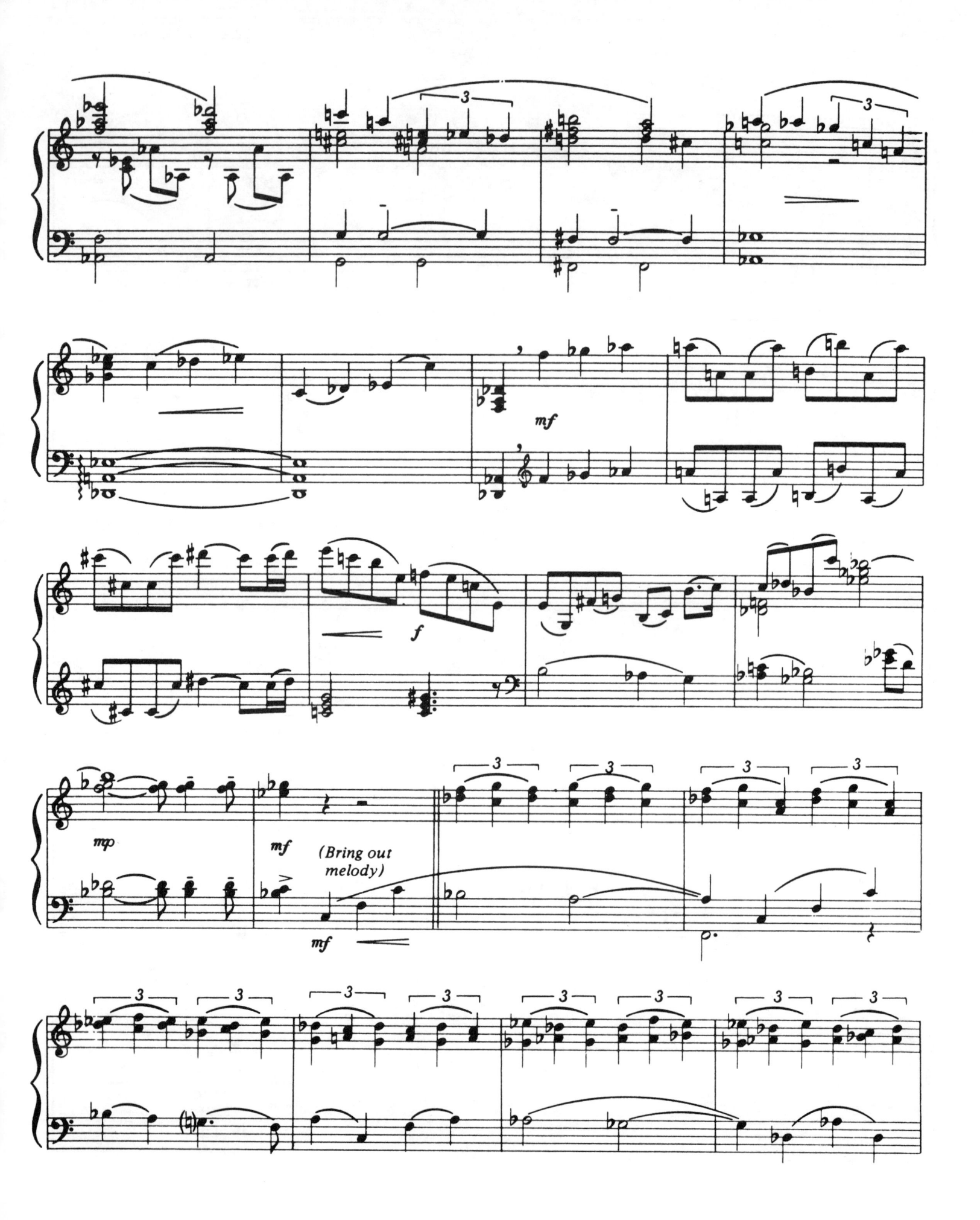
mf
f
mp
mf
(Bring out melody)
mf

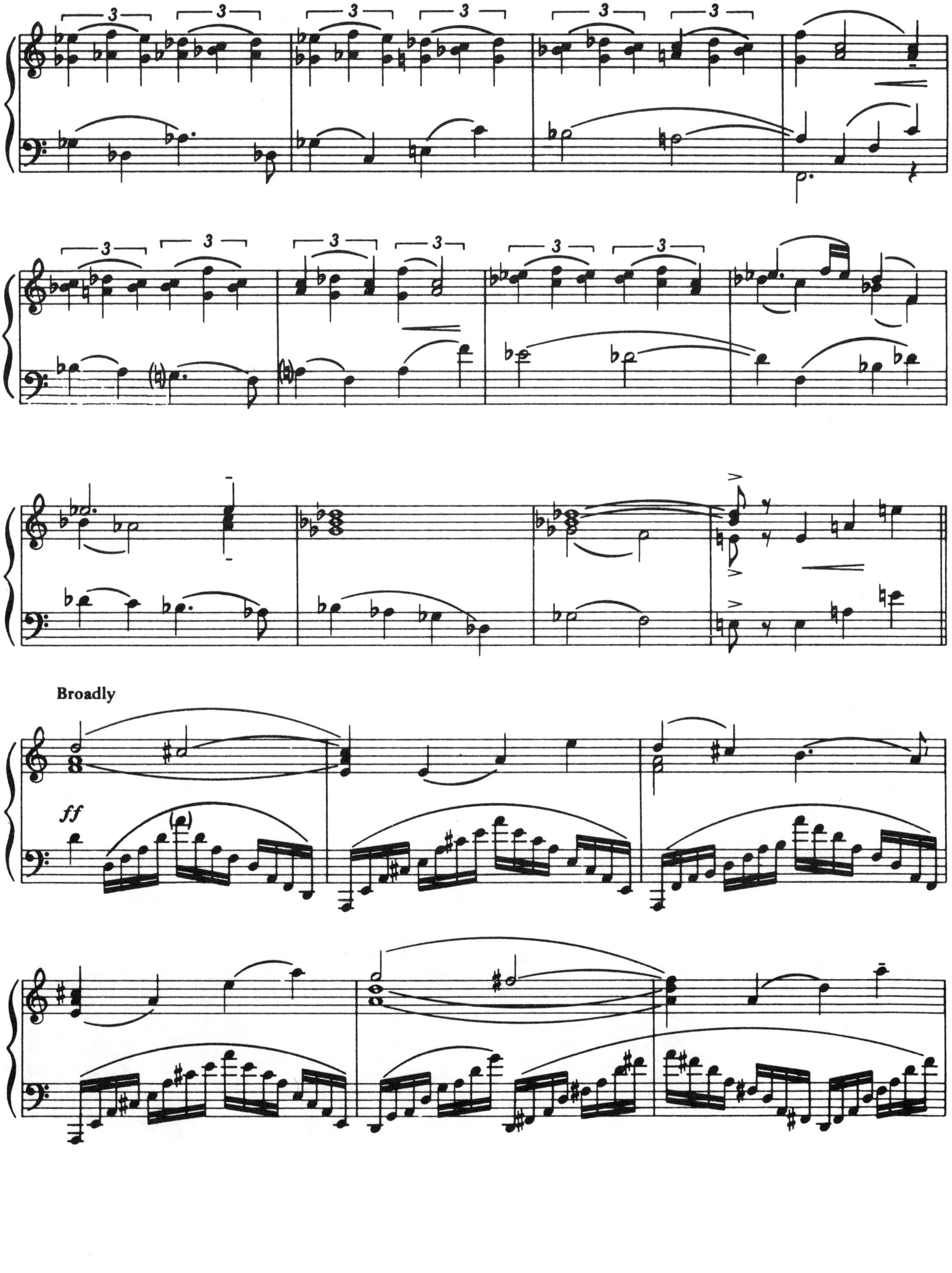
Broadly
ff

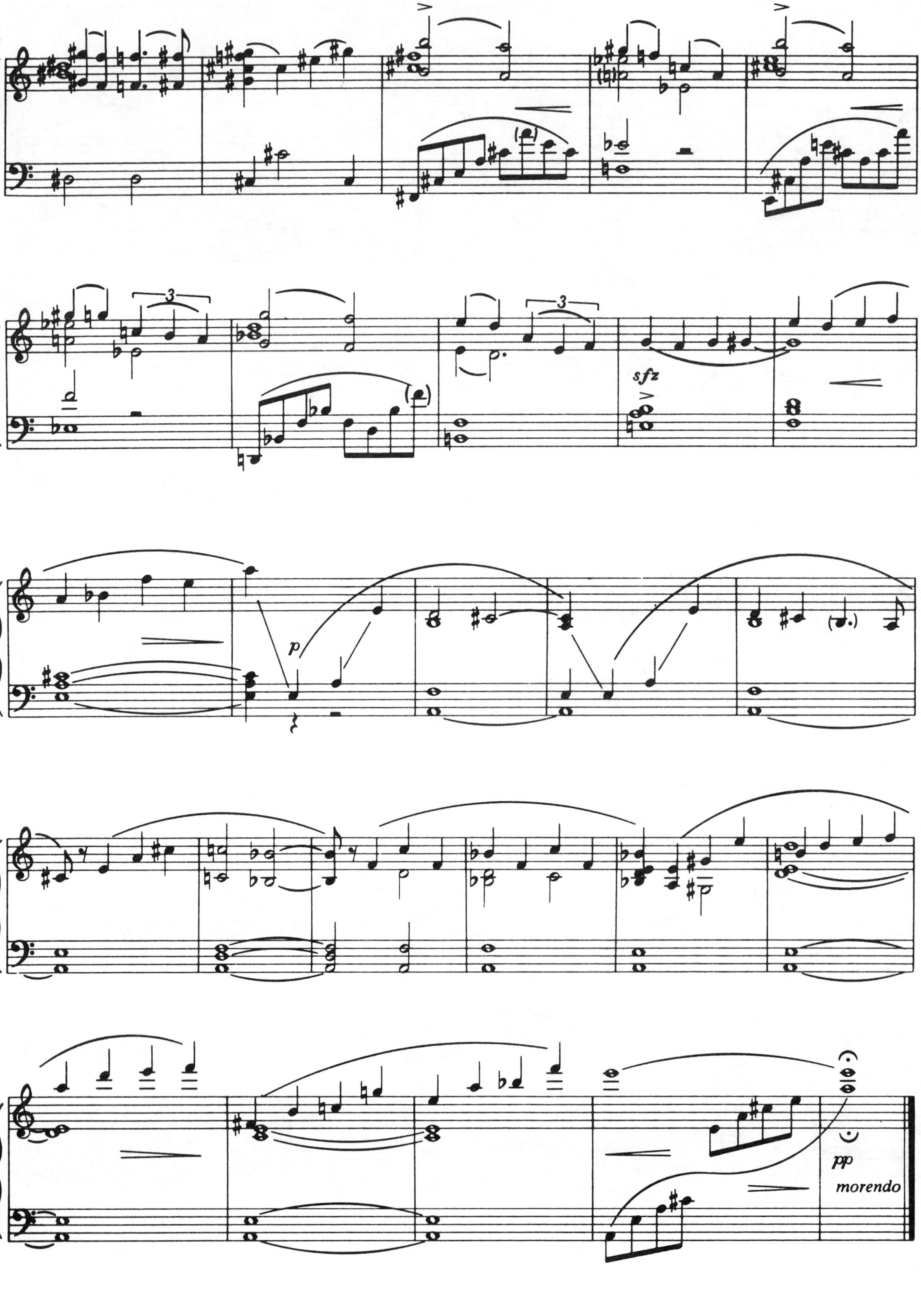
3
3
sfz
p
pp
morendo

THE EMPEROR

From the Lucasfilm Ltd. Production - A Twentieth Century-Fox Release "RETURN OF THE JEDI"

Music by
JOHN WILLIAMS

Dramatico

with pedal throughout

© 1983 BANTHA MUSIC
All rights administered by WARNER-TAMERLANE PUBLISHING CORP.
All Rights Reserved

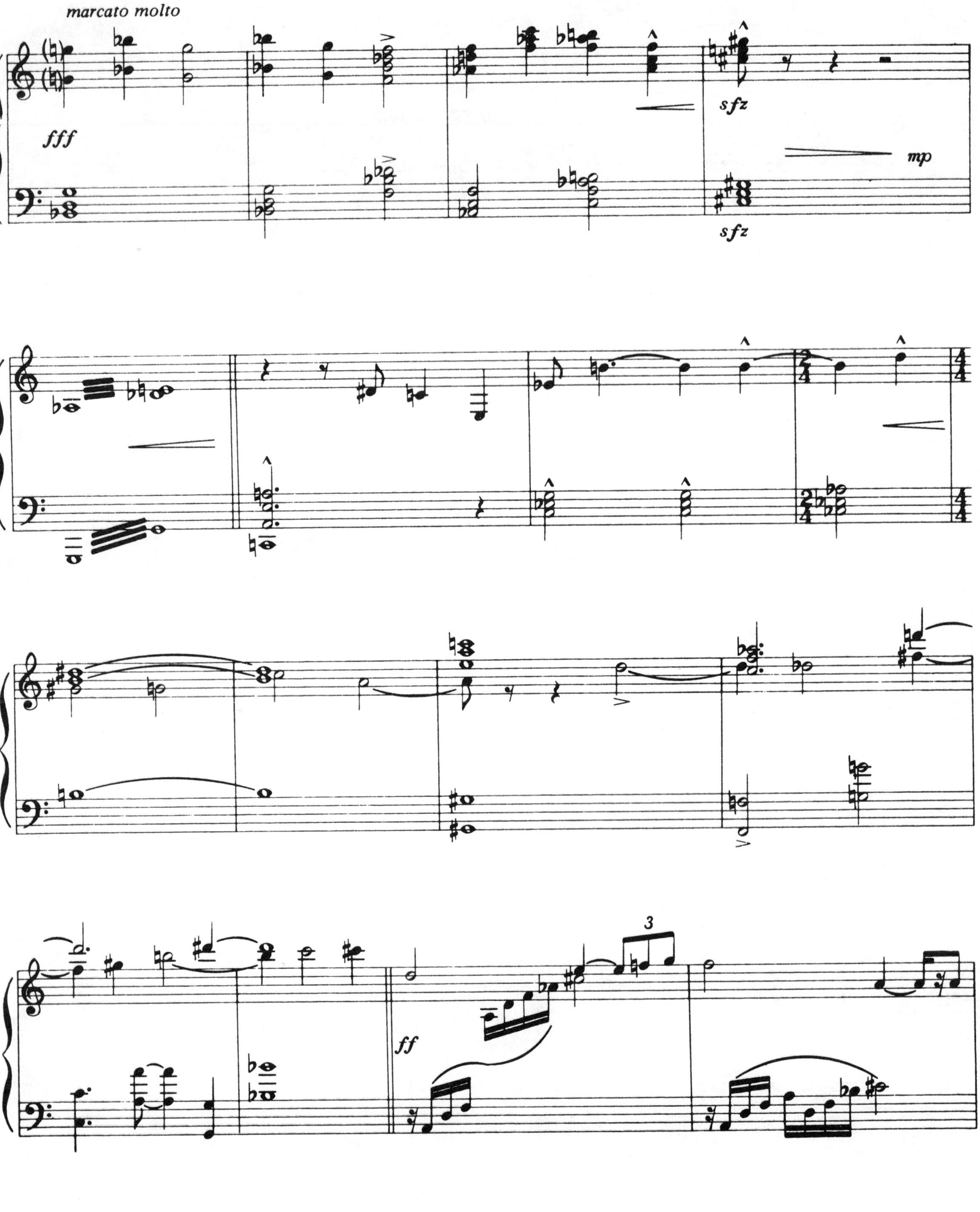
marcato molto
fff
sfz
mp
sfz
3
ff

59

THEME FROM E.T.
(The Extra Terrestrial)

By John Williams

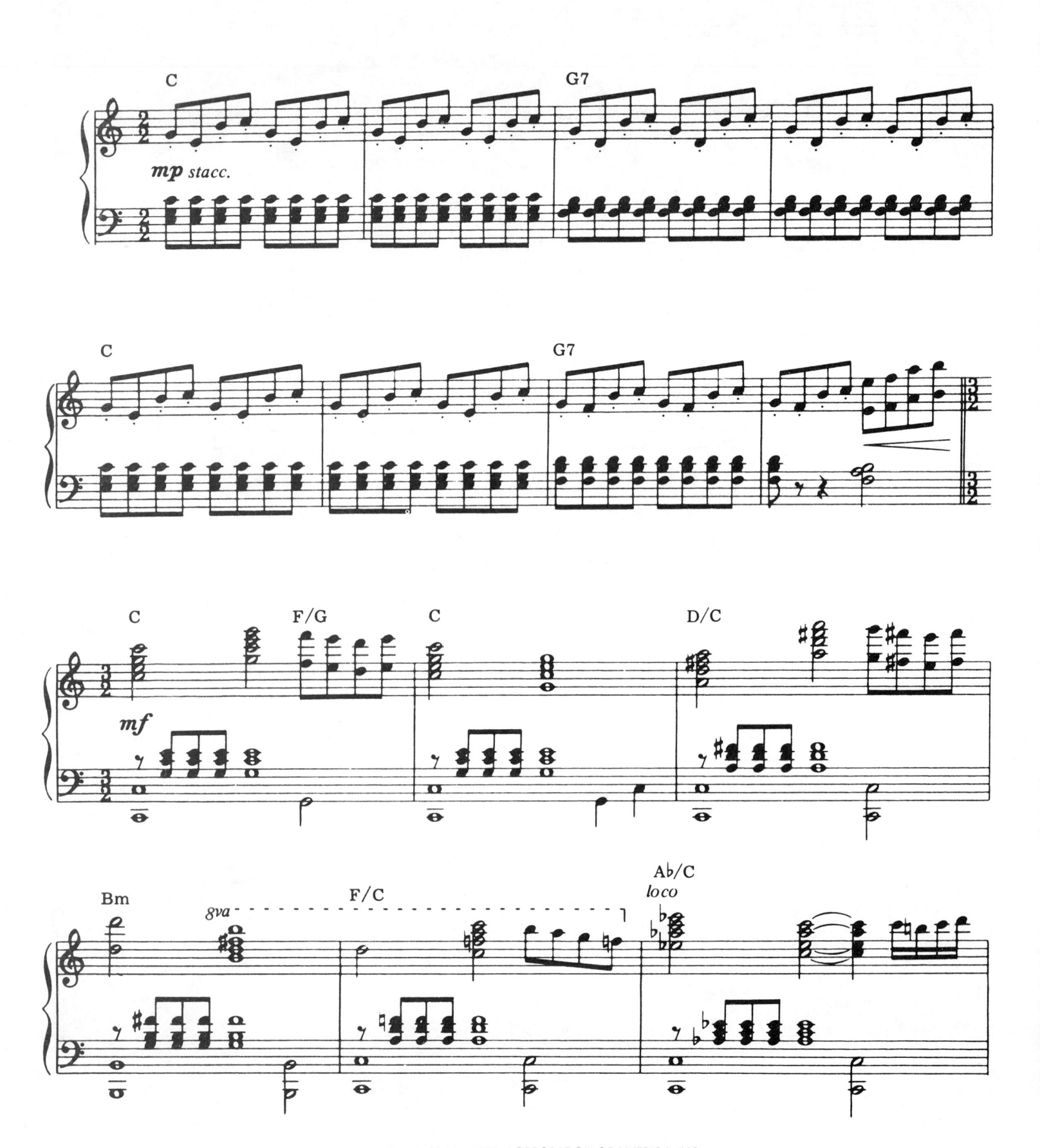

A♭/D
Cmaj7
C
stacc.
C
stacc.
D/C
(simile)
Bm
F/C
stacc.
A♭
A♭
C
Fdim
mp
G
B
mf
Fdim
G
B
mf
E♭7
mp
F♯m
F
mf

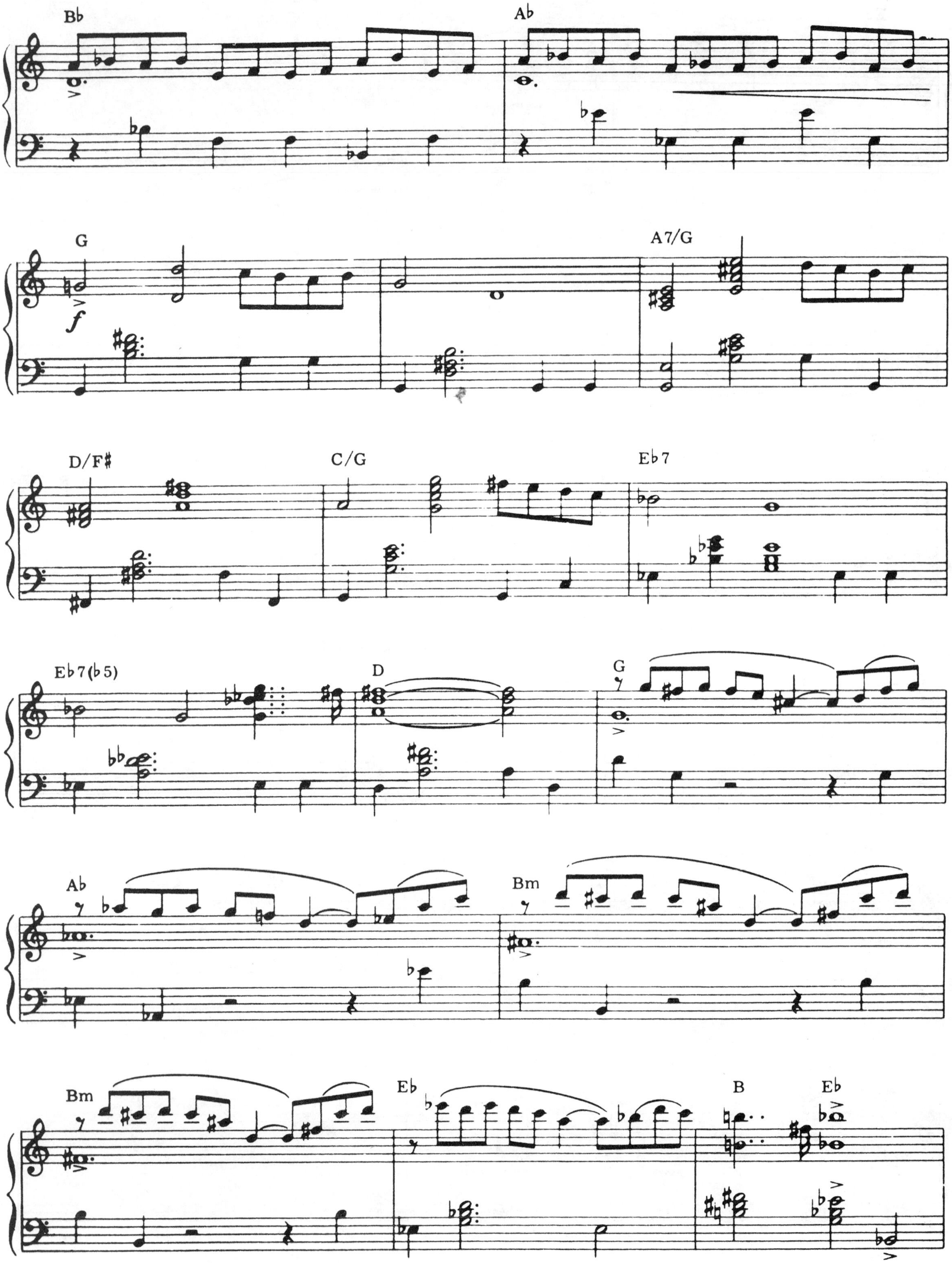
B♭
A♭
G
f
A7/G
D/F♯
C/G
E♭7
E♭7(♭5)
D
G
A♭
Bm
Bm
E♭
B
E♭

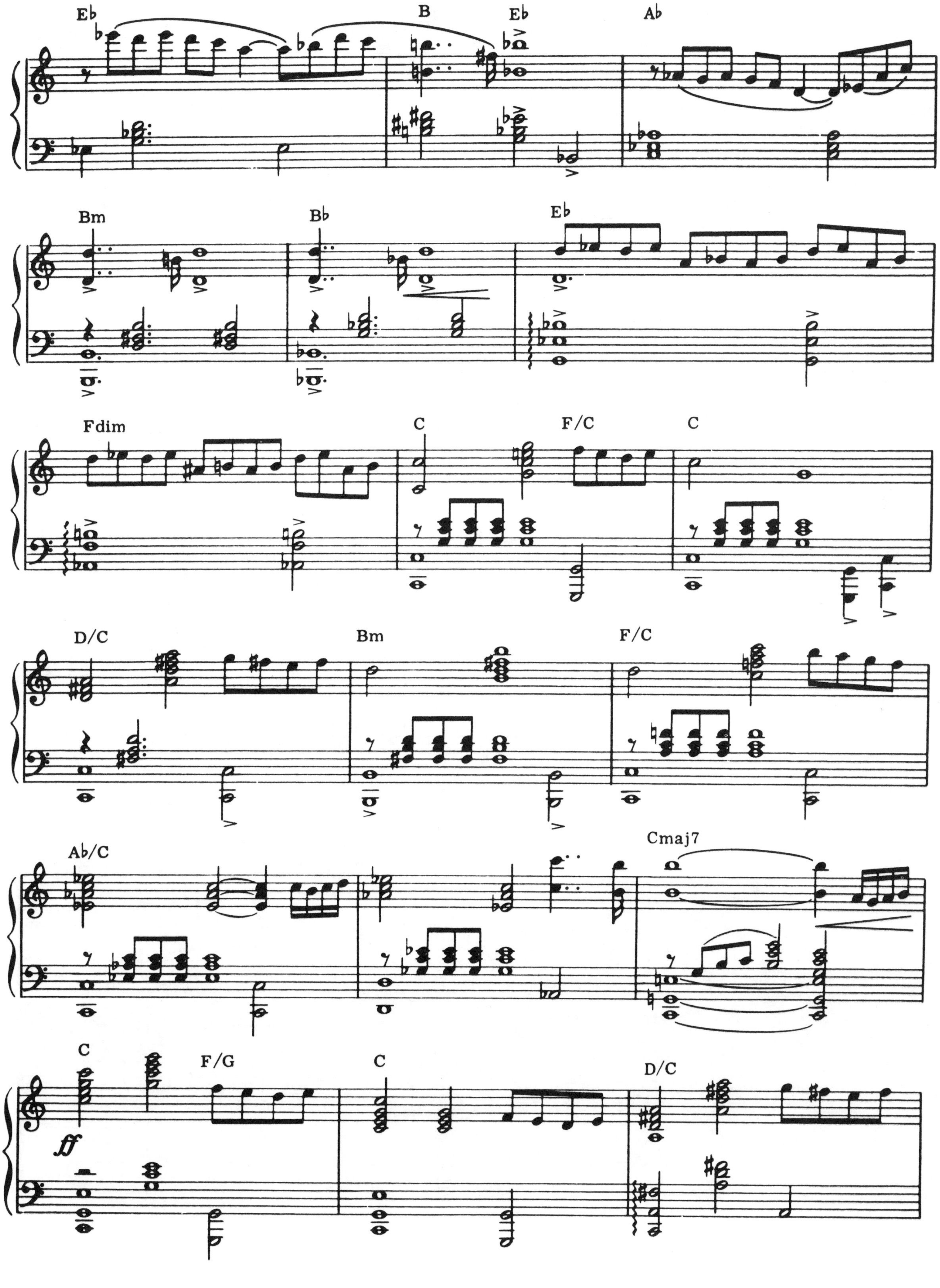
Eb
B
Eb
Ab
Bm
Bb
Eb
Fdim
C
F/C
C
D/C
Bm
F/C
Ab/C
Cmaj7
C
F/G
C
D/C
ff

Bm
F/C
Ab/C
G7 Tacet
sim.
rit.
G7 Tacet
C(no3)
ff
Ped.
(Tacet)
C(no3)
Tacet
Tacet
C(no3)
ff
rall.
Tacet
p
D7/C
C
mf
cresc.
Ped.

THEME FROM CLOSE ENCOUNTERS OF THE THIRD KIND

Music by JOHN WILLIAMS

Gmaj7
Em7
Gmaj7
Cmaj7
mp
Bm7
Cmaj7
cresc.
8va bassa
(loco)
Dmaj7
mf
Dmaj7/F♯
Fmaj 7
f
Dm7
ff
Gmaj7
mf

Gmaj7
Em7
mp
Gmaj7
Cmaj7
Bm7
Am7
mf cresc.
C/G
Fmaj7
f
C♯m7
sfz
ff
gliss.
8va bassa
(loco)

Cmaj7
sfz
ff
8va bassa
(loco)
Am9
p
Em9
mp
E♭maj7(add 9)
mf
Dm11
D9
sfz

Gmaj7
Em7
ff
Gmaj7
f
Em7
Gmaj7
Fsus
Dsus
G(add 9)
rall.
ff
sfz
L. H.
mp
ritard
p

IF WE WERE IN LOVE

(From the MGM Motion Picture "YES, GEORGIO")

Words by
ALAN and MARILYN BERGMAN

Music by
JOHN WILLIAMS

Cm7 3fr.
F7
Bbmaj7
Bb6
Bbmaj7
Bb6
if we were in love?
And could we seem
an - y
Eb/Bb
Cm/Bb 4fr.
F13
Bbmaj7
Eb/Bb
clos - er to a star?
Could we feel more than we're feel - ing,
C/Bb
Bbmaj7
Fm7
Ab/Bb 4fr.
dream more than we're dream - ing,
if we were in love?
Ebmaj9
Em9
A13
If we were in love,
you'd think we'd know
it. When

peo-ple are in love, _____ they tend to show it. Could the days fly _____ an-y fast-er than they do? _____ Could I be more than I'm be-ing, see more than I'm see-ing, when I look at you? _____ Could the sun shine _____ an-y brighter up above? If the wonder of a kiss is as wonderful as this, just imagine how you'd love me, how I'd love you, if we were in love!

allarg.

cresc.

f

PRINCESS LEIA'S THEME

From the Lucasfilm Ltd. Production - A Twentieth Century-Fox Release "RETURN OF THE JEDI"

Music by
JOHN WILLIAMS

Freely
Adim
mp
B/F#
L.H.
f
Edim
E7(♭9)
mp
A/E
f
mf
2. Gm7
Asus
A
rit.
D
f
a tempo
Gm6/D
D
Gm/D
D
rit.
mp
Freely
Gm6
rit.
8va
8va

RAIDERS MARCH

By
JOHN WILLIAMS

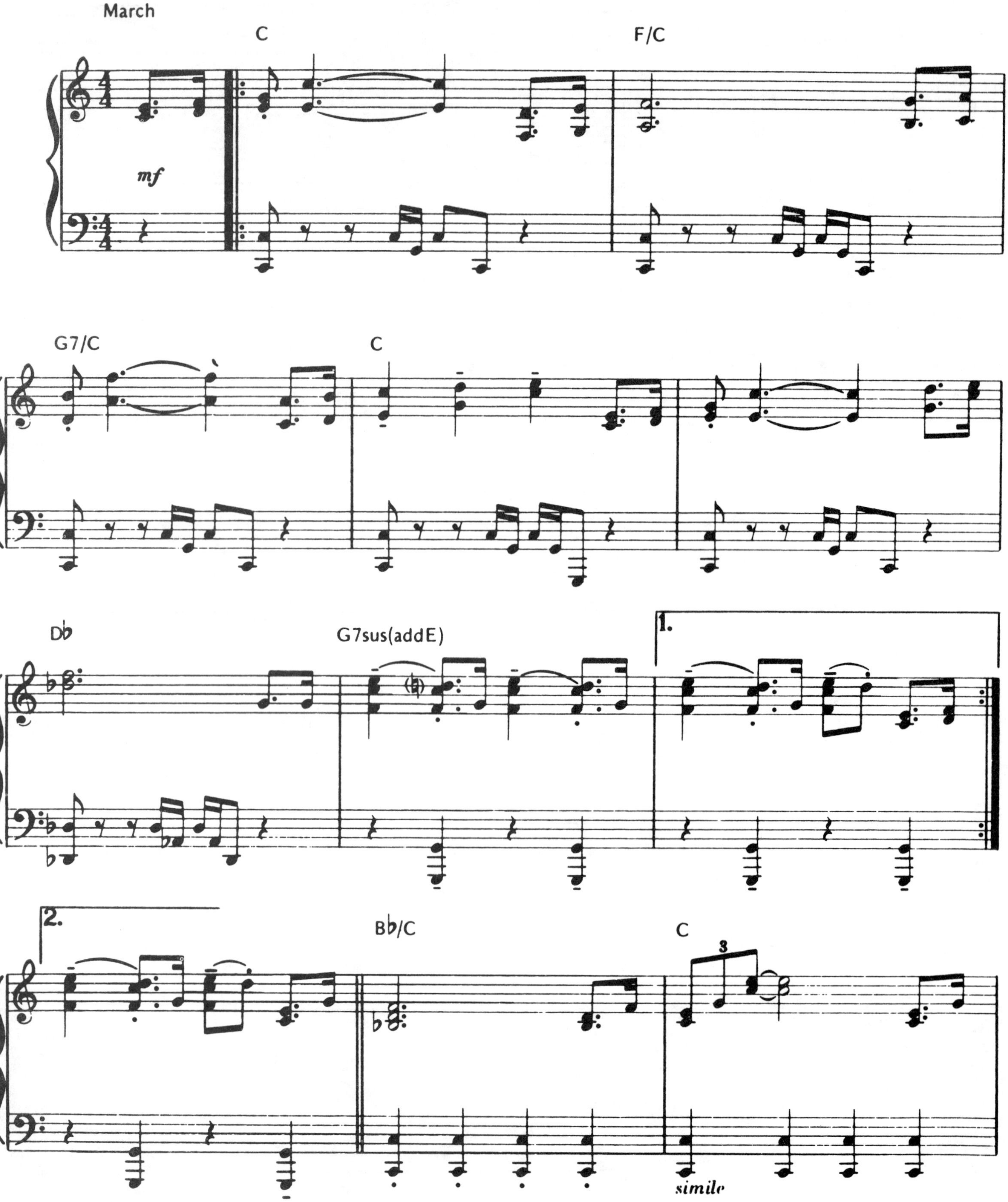

77

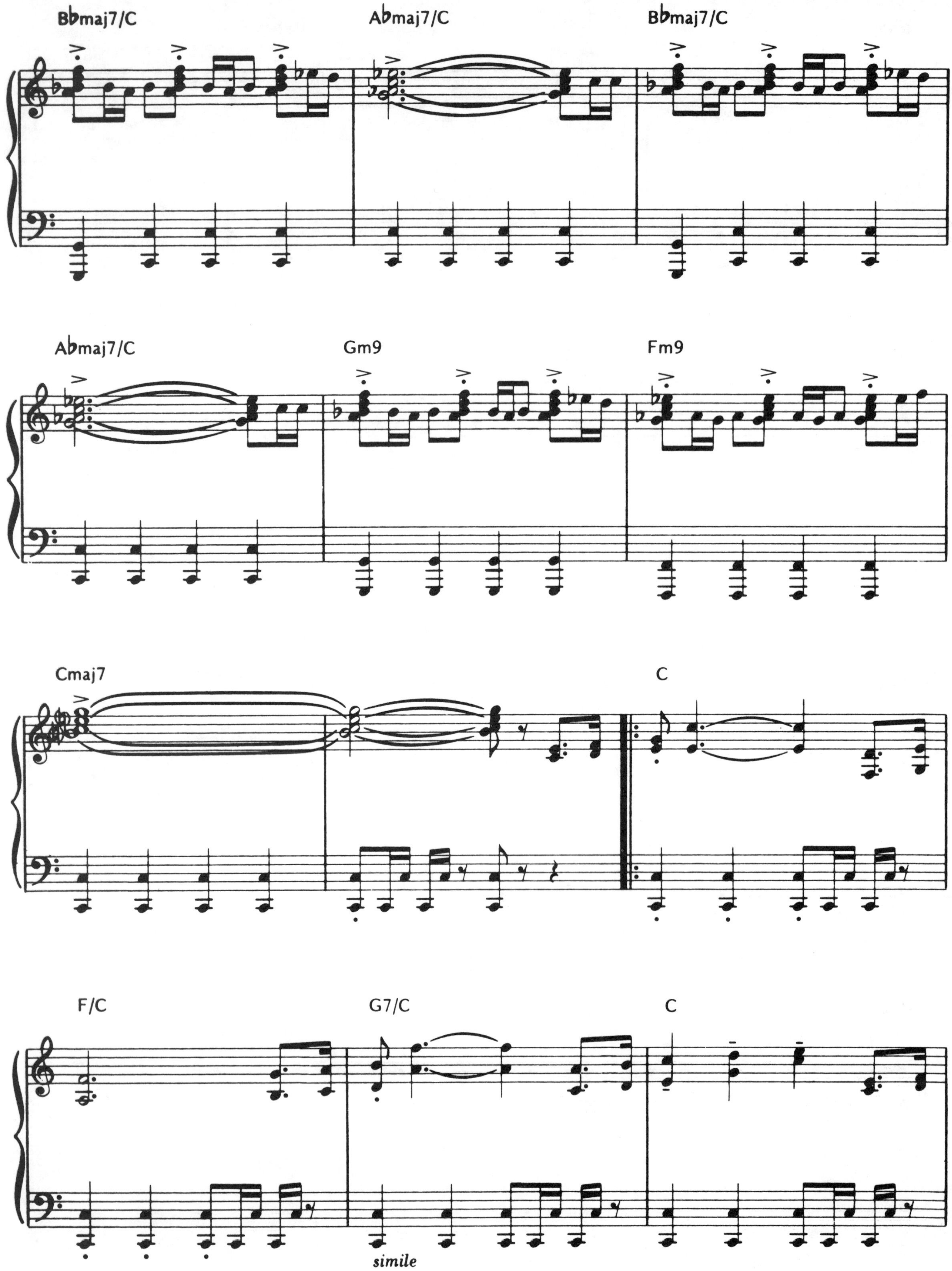
B♭maj7/C
A♭maj7/C
B♭maj7/C
A♭maj7/C
Gm9
Fm9
Cmaj7
C
F/C
G7/C
C
simile

D♭
G7sus(Add E)
1.
2.
C
Gm9
Cmaj7
Gm9
Cmaj7
A♭maj7/G
B♭maj7/G
Cmaj7
N.C.
8va bassa

HAN SOLO RETURNS
(At The Court of Jabba the Hutt)

From the Lucasfilm Ltd. Production - A Twentieth Century-Fox Release "RETURN OF THE JEDI"

Music by
JOHN WILLIAMS

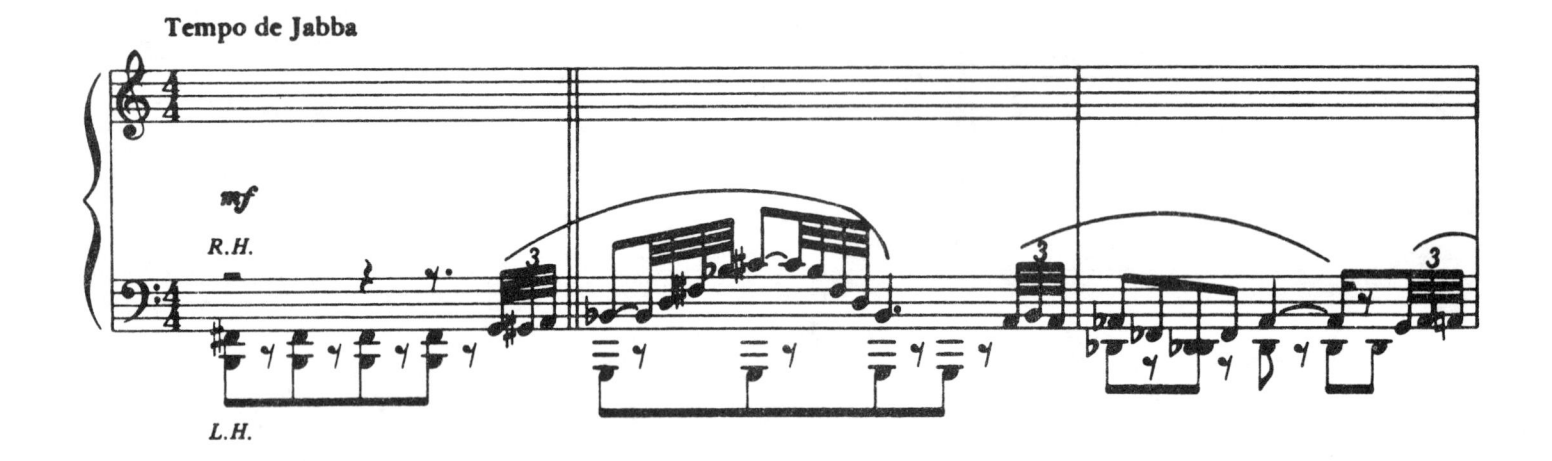

Tempo de Jabba

© 1983 BANTHA MUSIC
All rights administered by WARNER-TAMERLANE PUBLISHING CORP.
All Rights Reserved

81

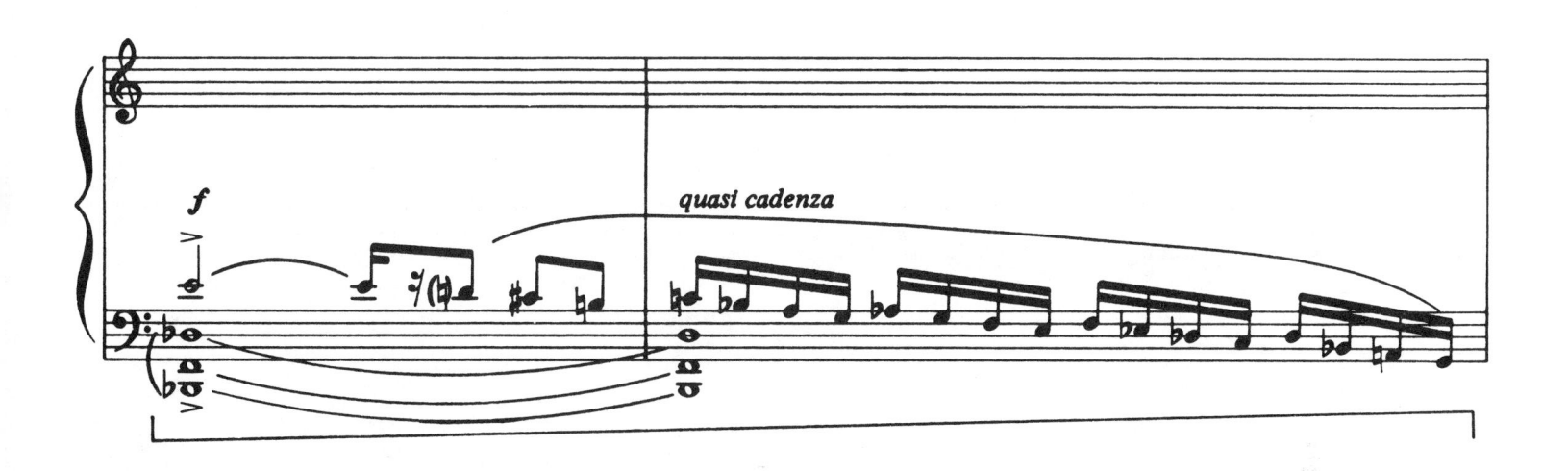

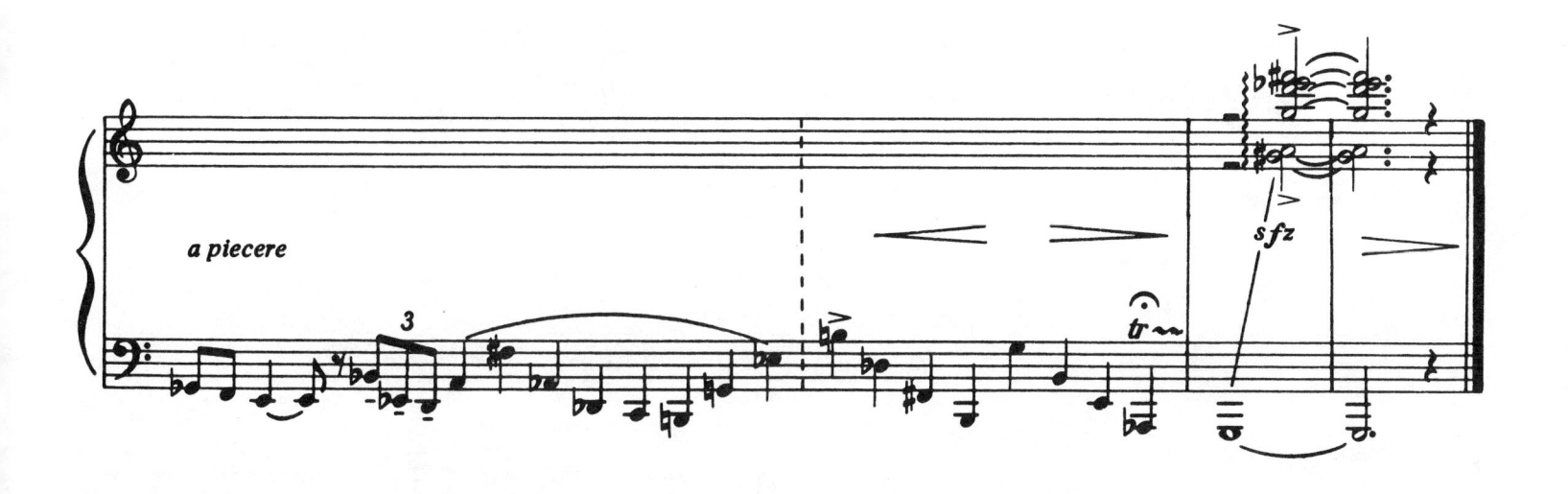

THE FOREST BATTLE

From the Lucasfilm Ltd. Production - A Twentieth Century-Fox Release "RETURN OF THE JEDI"

Music by
JOHN WILLIAMS

© 1983 BANTHA MUSIC
All rights administered by WARNER-TAMERLANE PUBLISHING CORP.
All Rights Reserved

83

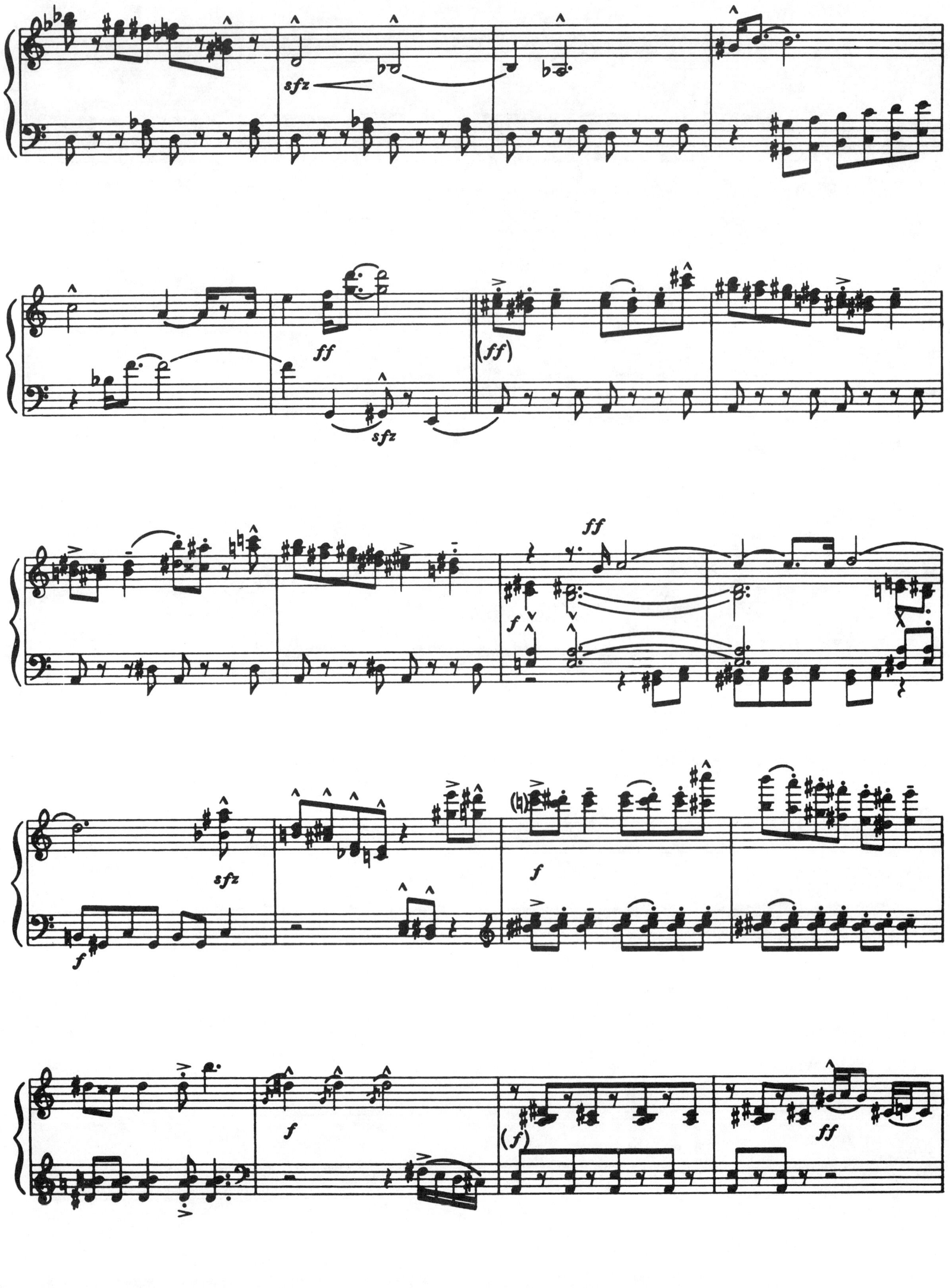
sfz
ff
sfz
(ff)
ff
f
sfz
f
f
f
(f)
ff

85

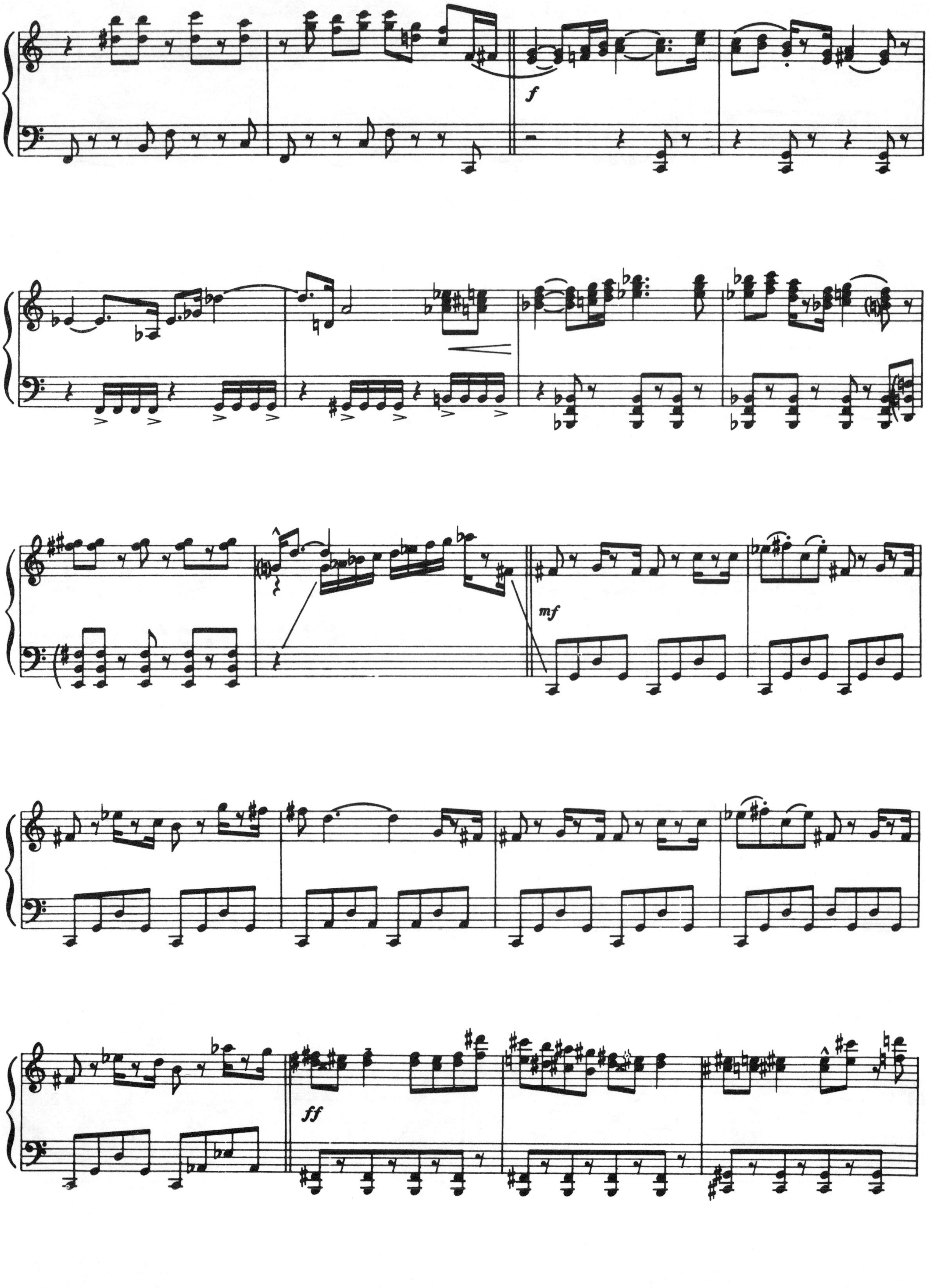
f
mf
ff

87

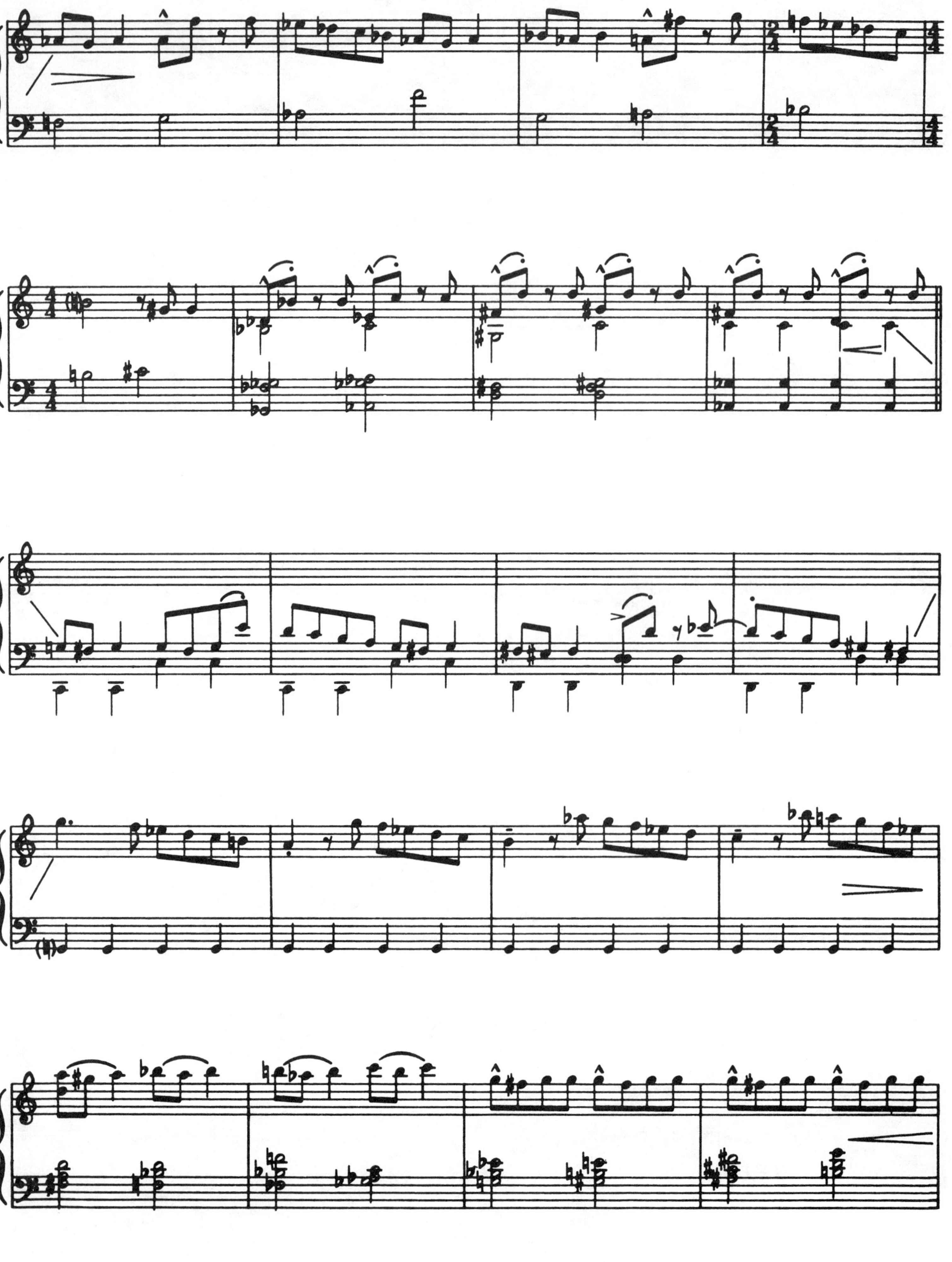

89

OLYMPIC FANFARE AND THEME
(Commissioned by the 1984 Los Angeles Olympic Organizing Committee)

By
JOHN WILLIAMS

Maestoso

© 1984 WARNER-TAMERLANE PUBLISHING CORP. & MARJER PUBLISHING CO. (BMI)
All rights administered by WARNER-TAMERLANE PUBLISHING CORP.
All Rights Reserved

91

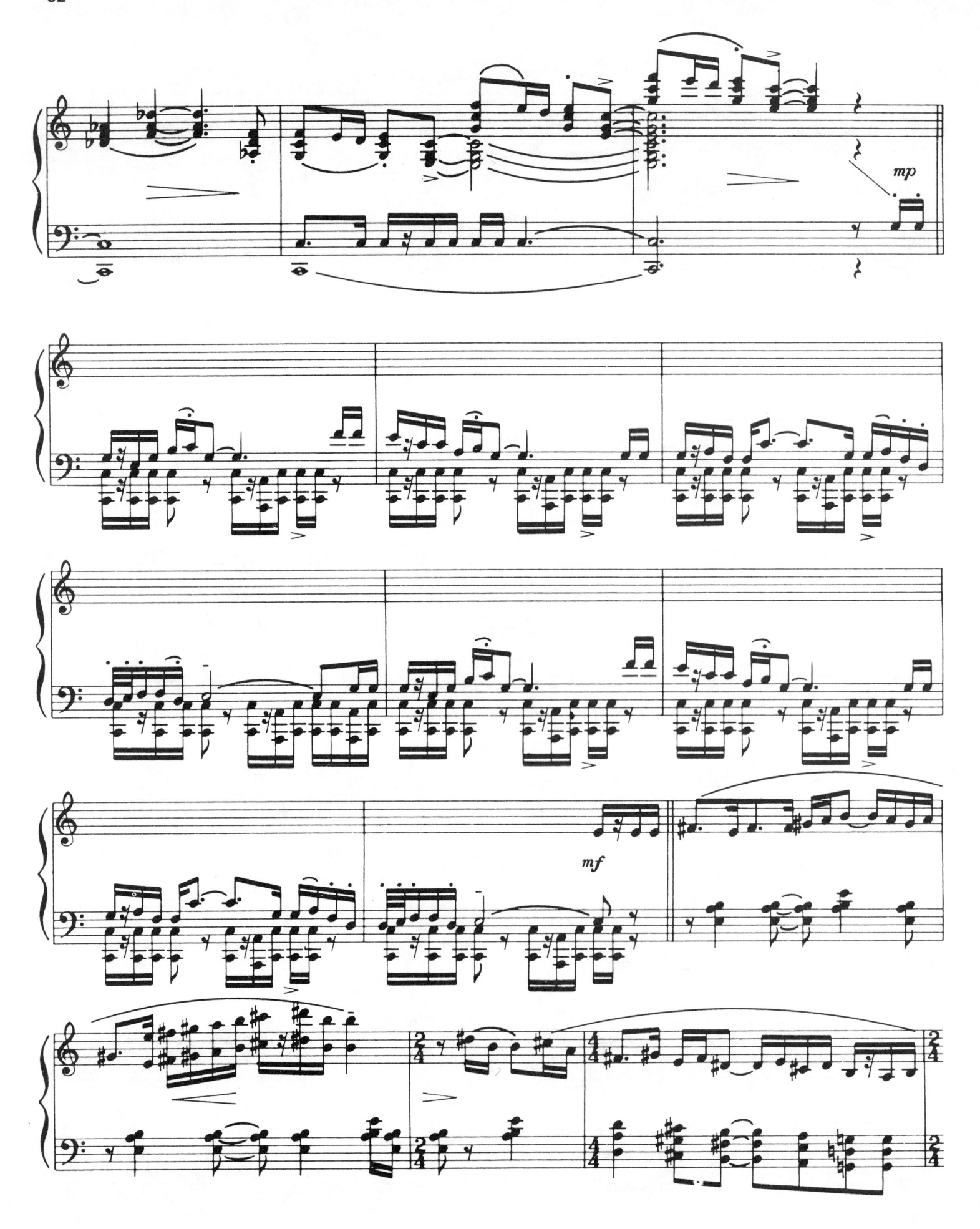
mp
mf

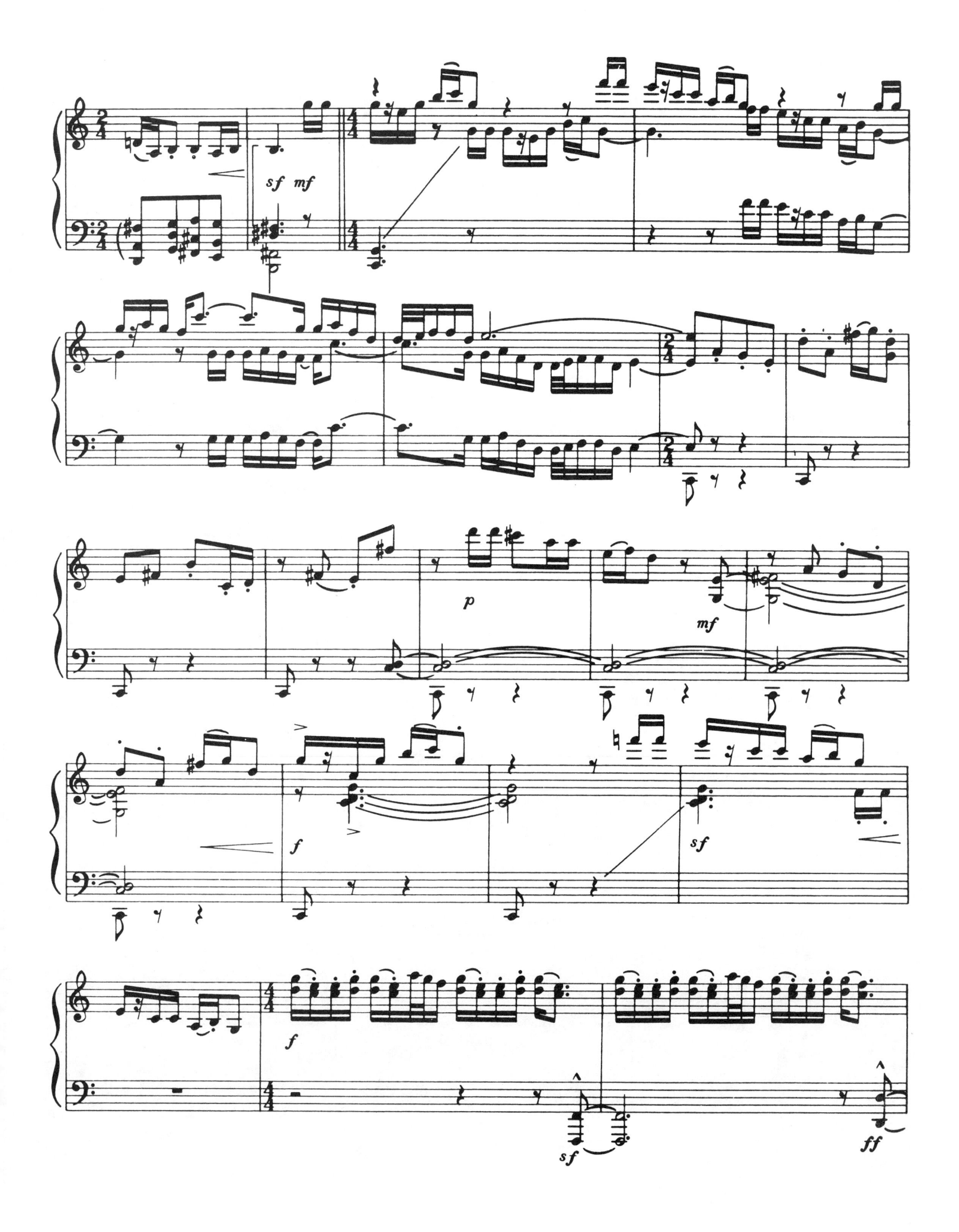
sf
mf
p
mf
f
sf
f
sf
ff

94

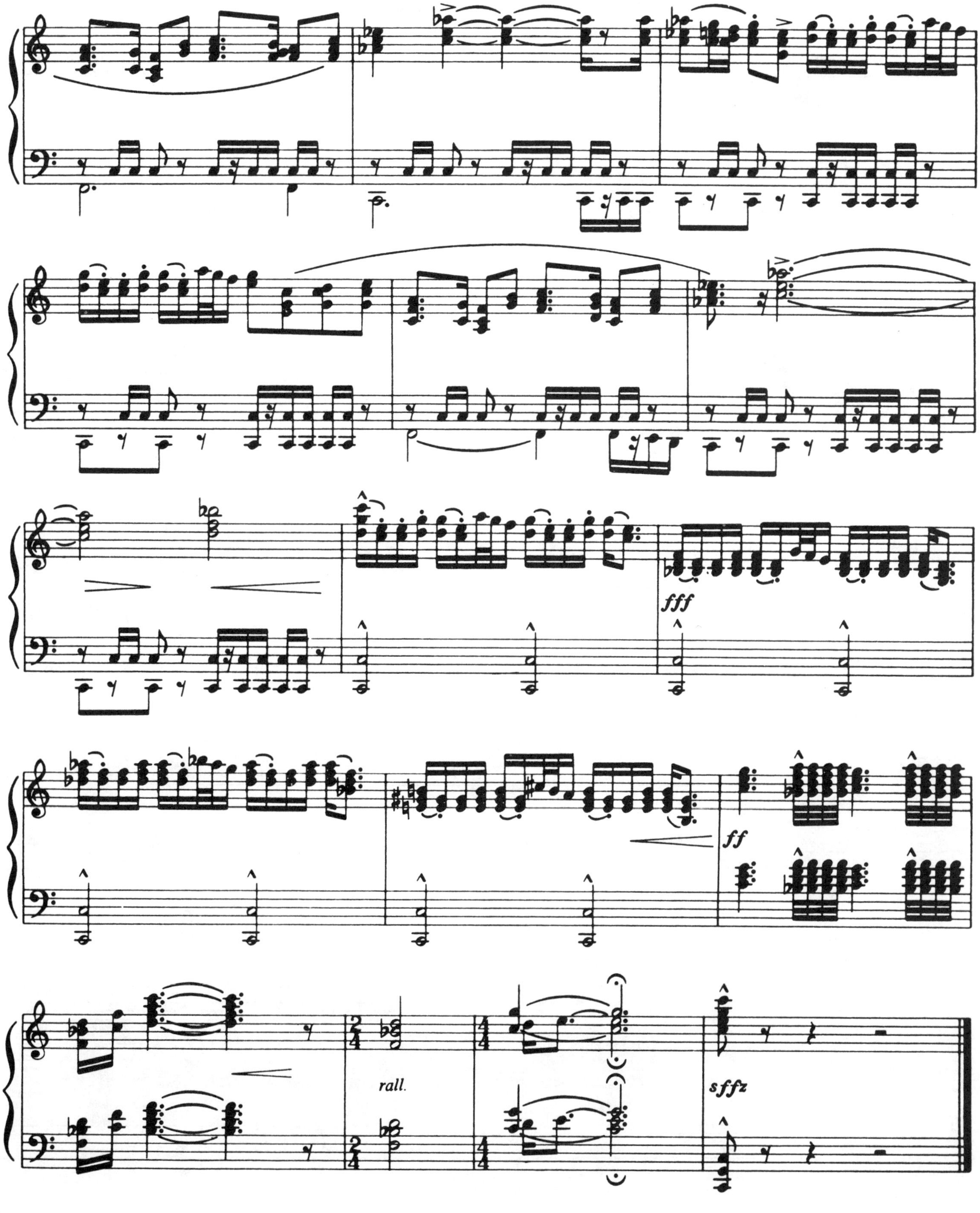
fff
ff
rall.
sffz

EWOK CELEBRATION

From the Lucasfilm Ltd. Production - A Twentieth Century-Fox Release "RETURN OF THE JEDI"

Ewokese Lyrics by
BEN BURTT

Original English Lyrics by
JOSEPH WILLIAMS

Music by
JOHN WILLIAMS

Bright Reggae beat

Yub nub, eee chop yub nub; ah
Free - dom, we got free - dom; and

toe meet toe pee - chee keene, g' - noop dock fling oh___ ah.___
now that we can be free, come on and cel - e - brate.___

Yah wah, eee chop yah wah;
Pow - er, we got pow - er;

© 1983 BANTHA MUSIC
All rights administered by WARNER-TAMERLANE PUBLISHING CORP.
All Rights Reserved

ah toe meet toe pee-chee keene, g'-noop dock
and now that we can be free, it's time to

fling oh ah. Coat-ee chah tu yub nub;
cel - e - brate. Cel - e - brate the free - dom;

coat-ee chah tu yah wah; coat-ee chah tu glo wah;
cel - e - brate the pow - er; cel - e - brate the glo - ry;

E♭ 3fr.
F
G
G
al - lay loo ta nuv.
cel - e - brate the love.
Glo - wah,
Pow - er,
eee chop
we got
f
Em
C
glo - wah;
pow - er;
ya glo - wah pee chu nee foam,
and now that we can be free,
Am
F
F♯
G
ah toot dee awe goon daa.
it's time to cel - e - brate.

Eb 3fr. F G
Coat - ee cha tu goo; (Yub nub!) coat - ee cha tu doo; (Yah - wah!)
Cel - e-brate the light; (Free - dom!) cel - e-brate the might; (Pow - er!)
coat - ee cha tu too; (Ya chaa!) al - lay loo ta nuv,
cel - e-brate the fight; (Glo - ry!) cel - e-brate the love.
To Coda
al - lay loo ta nuv,
cel - e-brate the love,
al - lay loo ta nuv.
cel - e-brate the love.

G
Em
Glo - wah, eee chop glo - wah. Ya
Glo - ry, we found glo - ry. The
C
Am
F
F#
G
glo - wah pee chu nee foam, ah toot dee awe goon daa.
pow - er showed us the light, and now we all live free.
D. S. al Coda
Coda
E♭
3fr.
F
G
al - lay loo ta nuv.
cel - e - brate the love.
ff

CELEBRATION FANFARE
(In Honor of the 150th Anniversary of the City of Houston)

By
JOHN WILLIAMS

© 1989 MARJER PUBLISHING CO.
All rights administered by WARNER-TAMERLANE PUBLISHING CORP.
All Rights Reserved

102

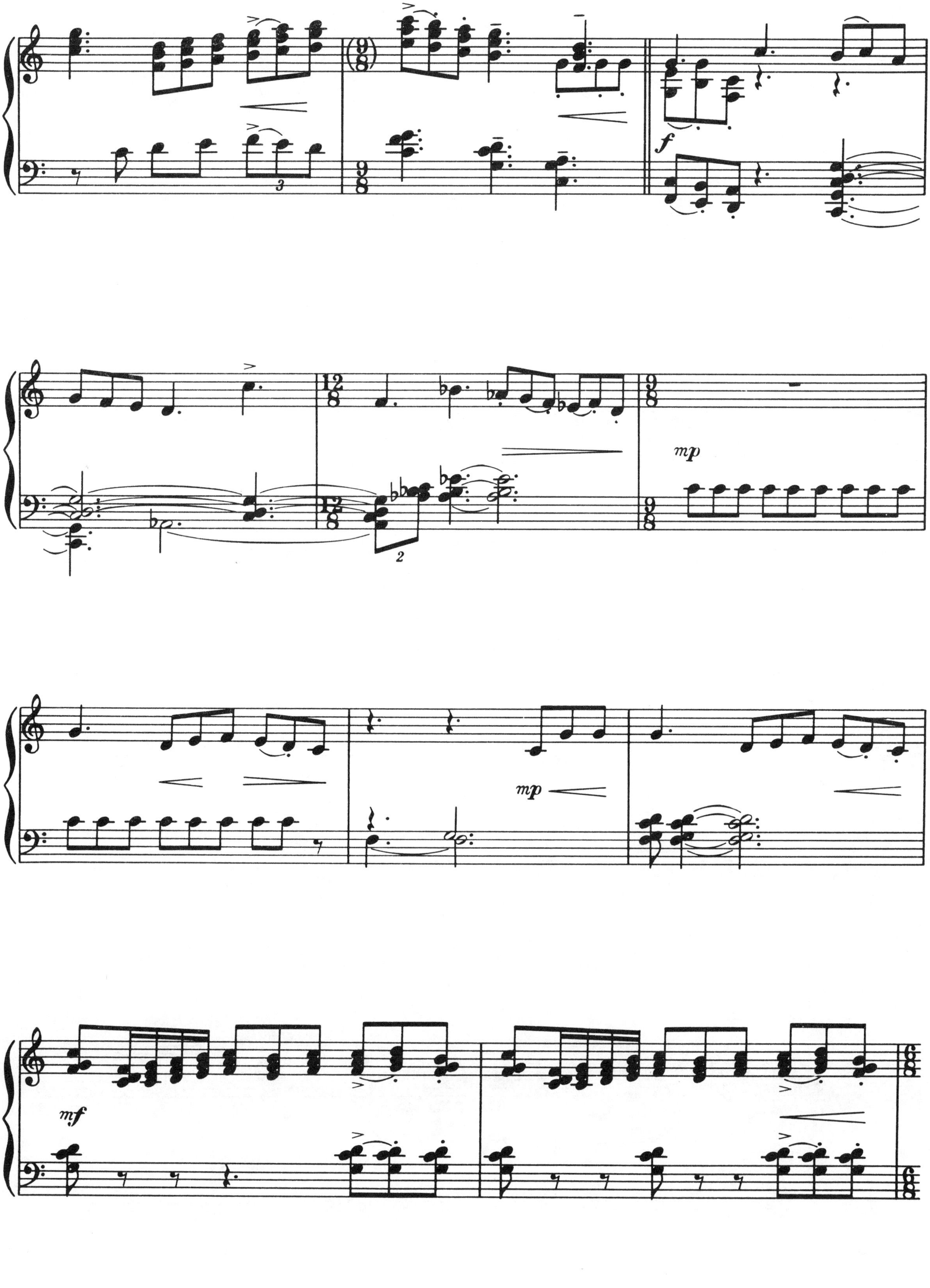
f
mp
mp
mf

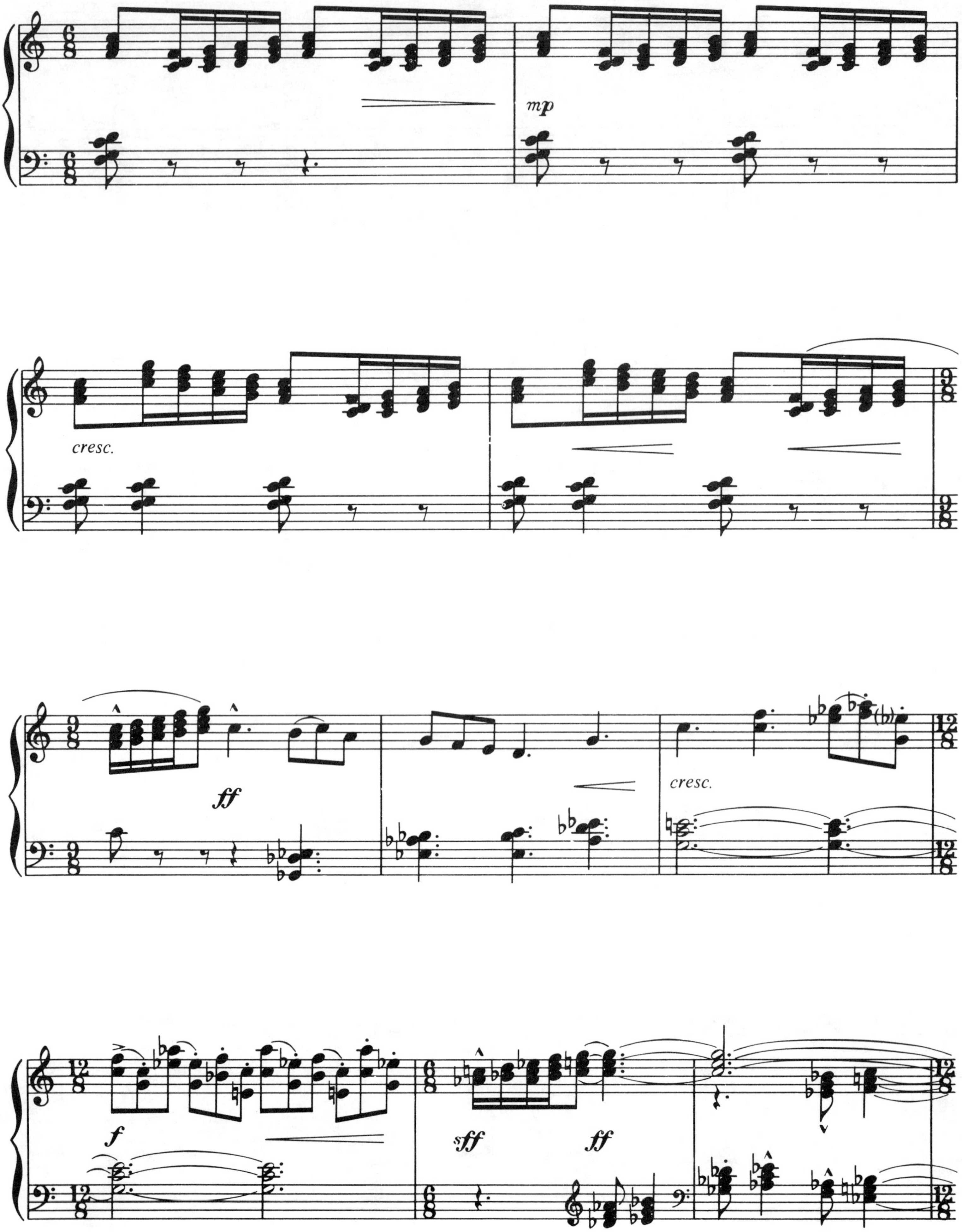
mp
cresc.
ff
cresc.
f
sff
ff

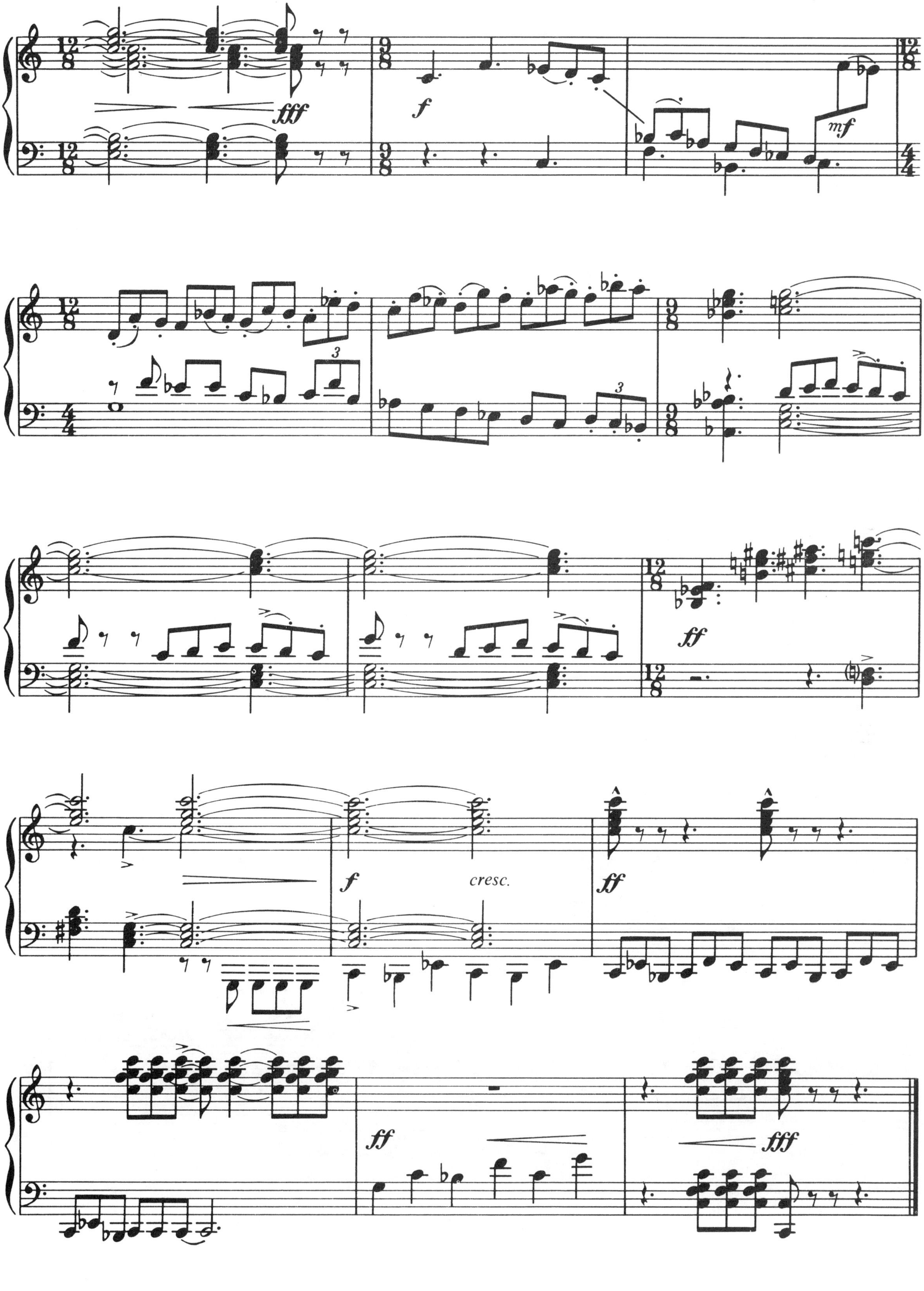
fff
f
mf
ff
f
cresc.
ff
ff
fff

PARADE OF THE EWOKS

From the Lucasfilm Ltd. Production - A Twentieth Century-Fox Release "RETURN OF THE JEDI"

Music by
JOHN WILLIAMS

© 1983 BANTHA MUSIC
All rights administered by WARNER-TAMERLANE PUBLISHING CORP.
All Rights Reserved

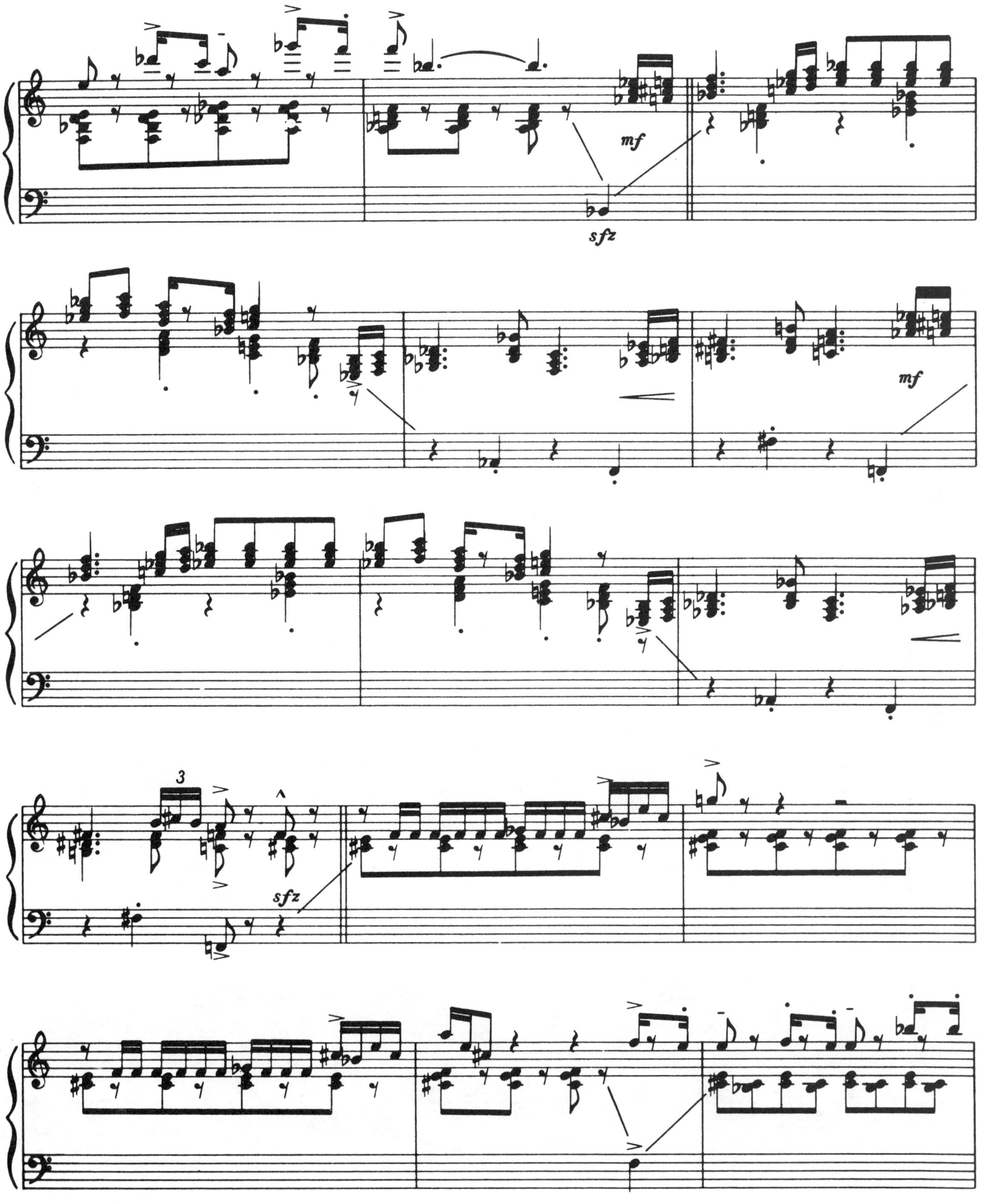

mf
sfz
mf
3
sfz

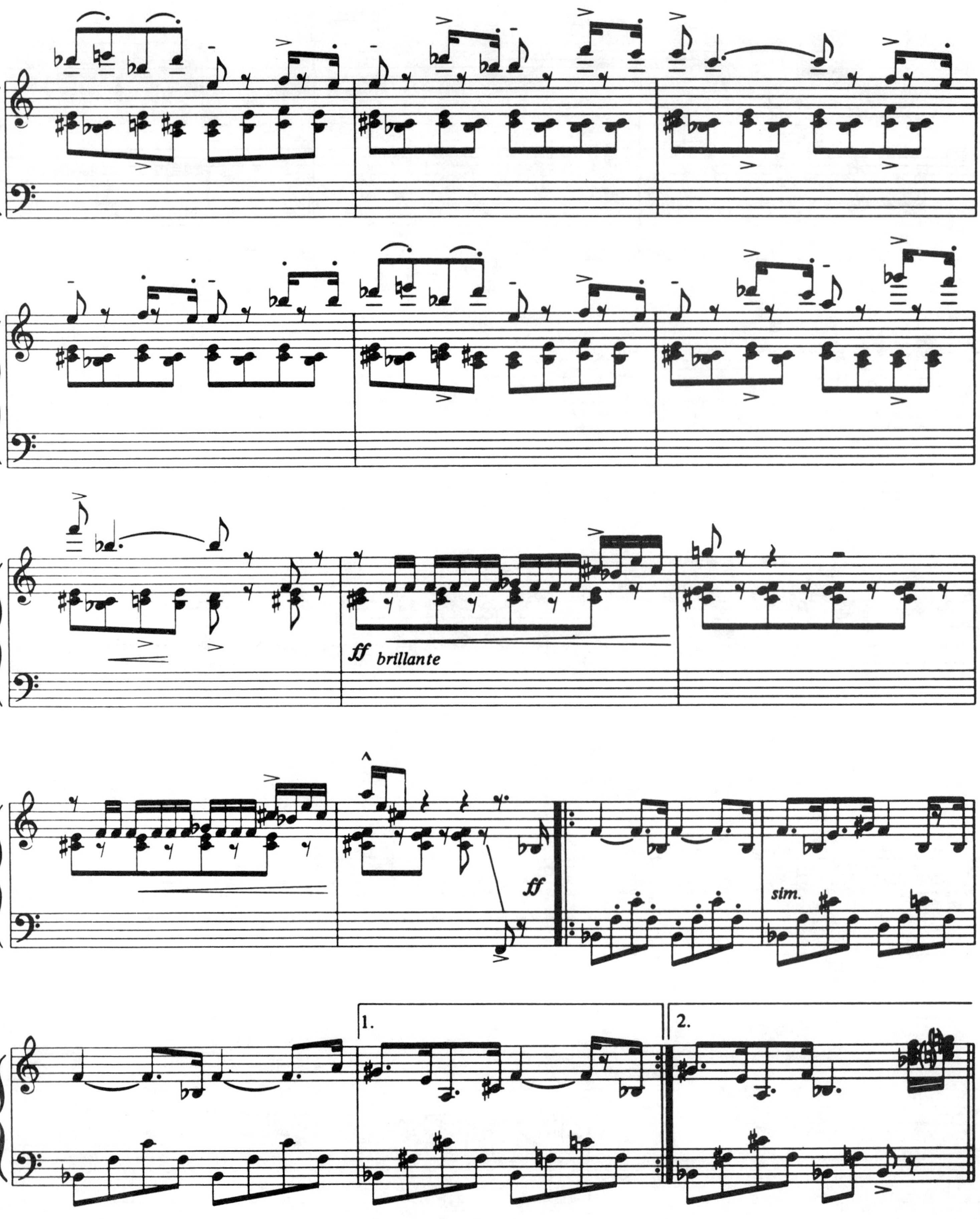

ff brillante
ff
sim.
1.
2.

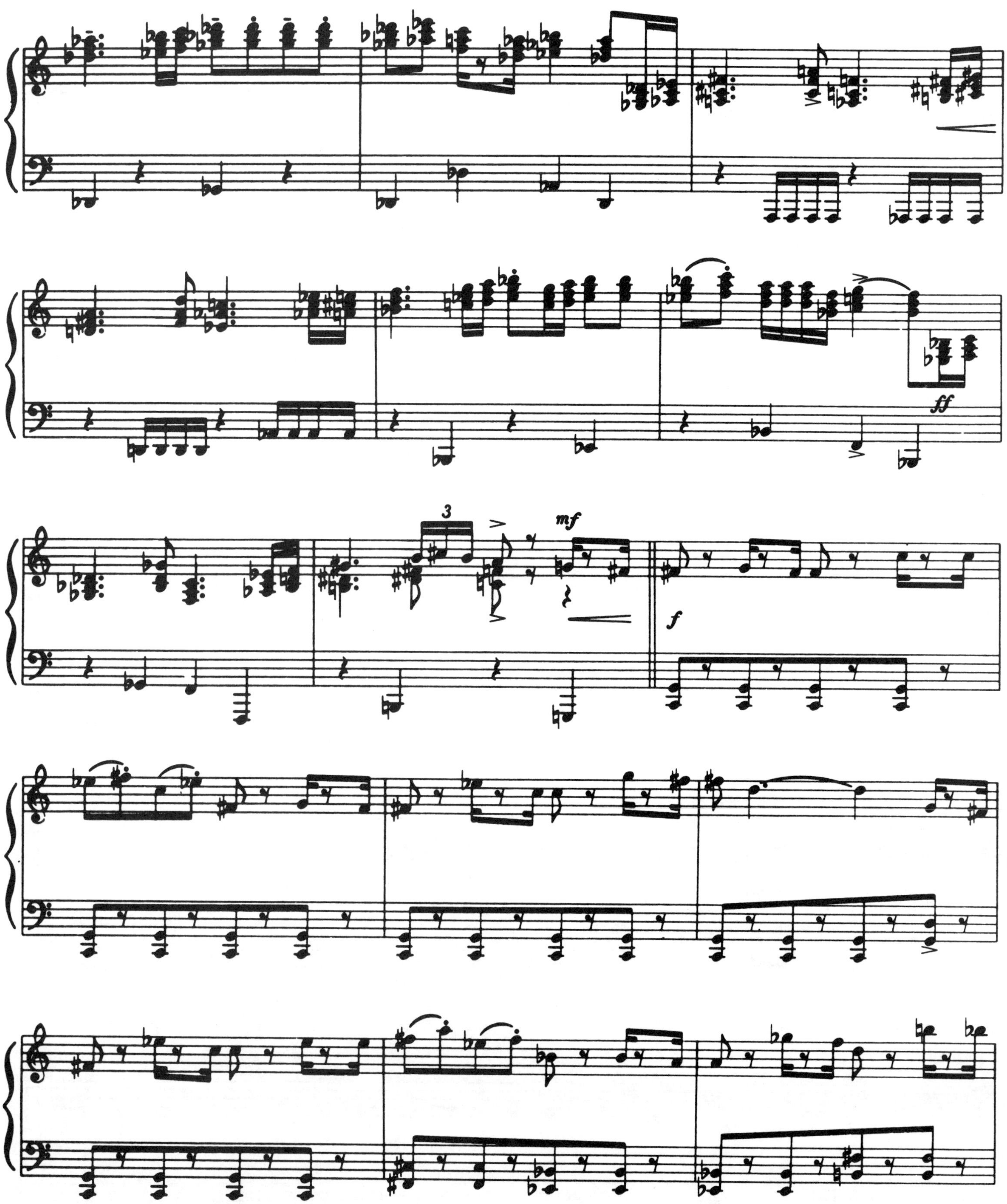
ff
3
mf
f

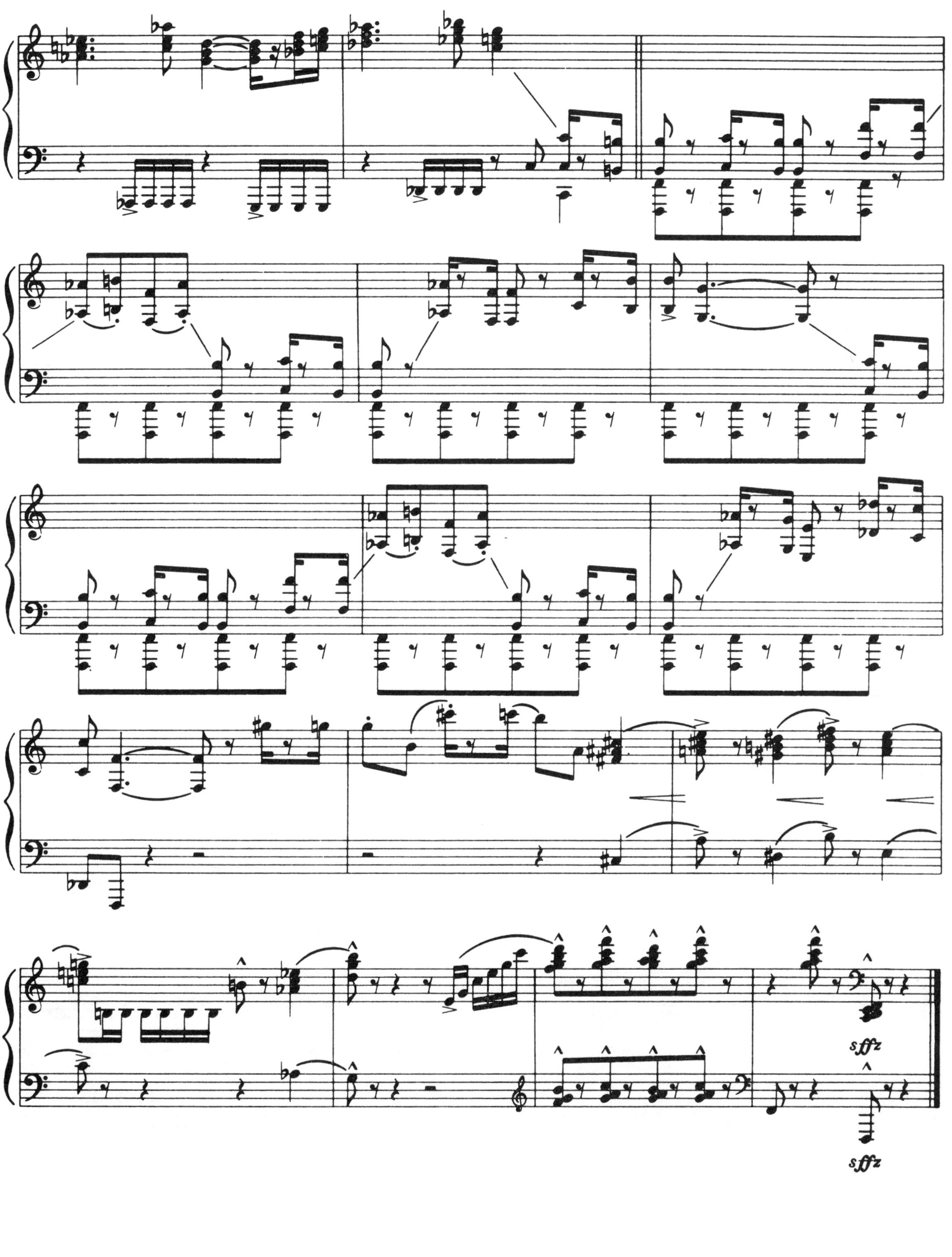
sffz
sffz

THE MISSION THEME
From NBC News

By JOHN WILLIAMS

© 1985 LIVING MUSIC, INC. and DEEP DELL MUSIC
All rights administered by EMI BLACKWOOD MUSIC INC. and EMI APRIL MUSIC INC.
All Rights Reserved

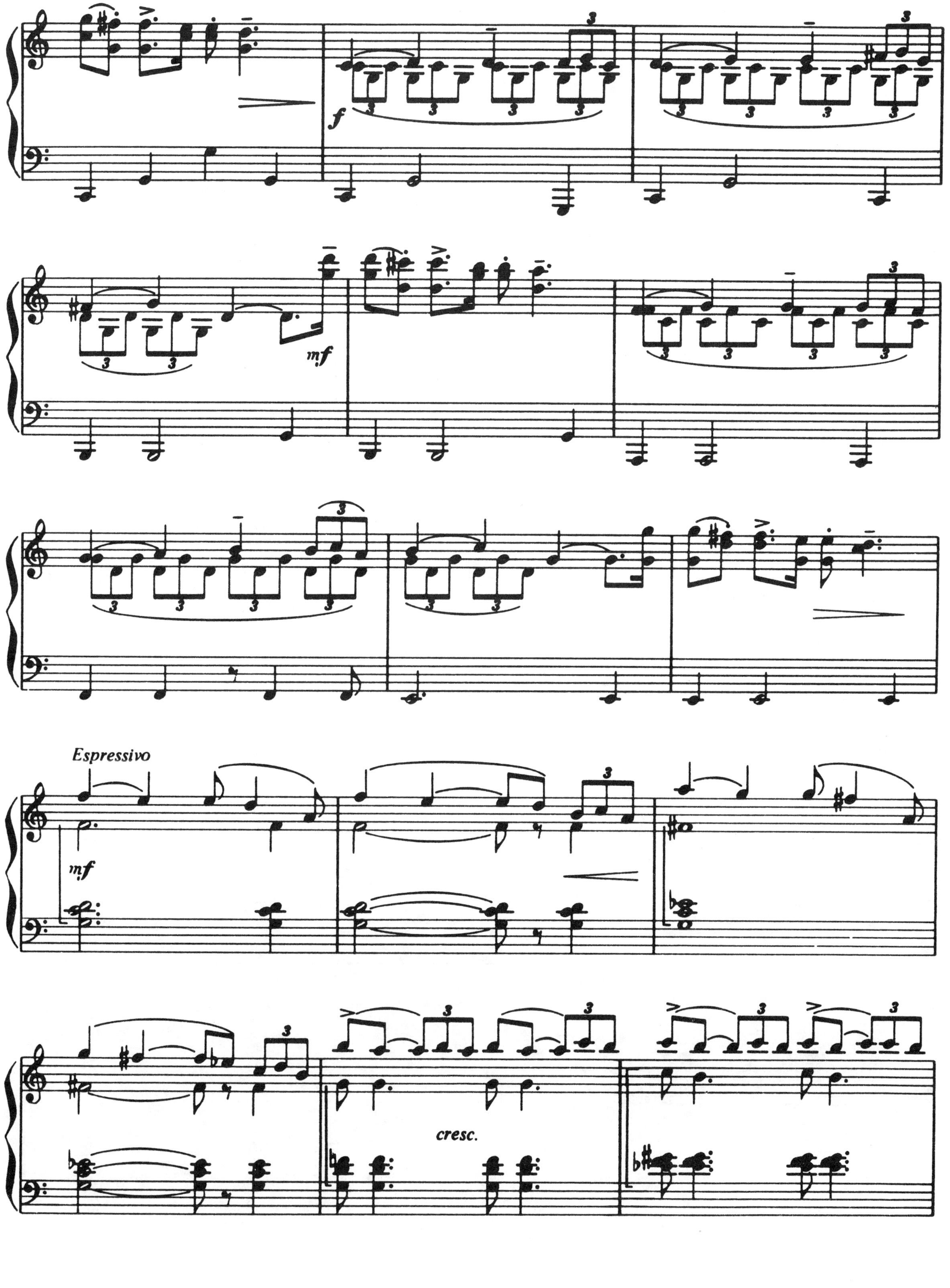
f
mf
Espressivo
mf
cresc.

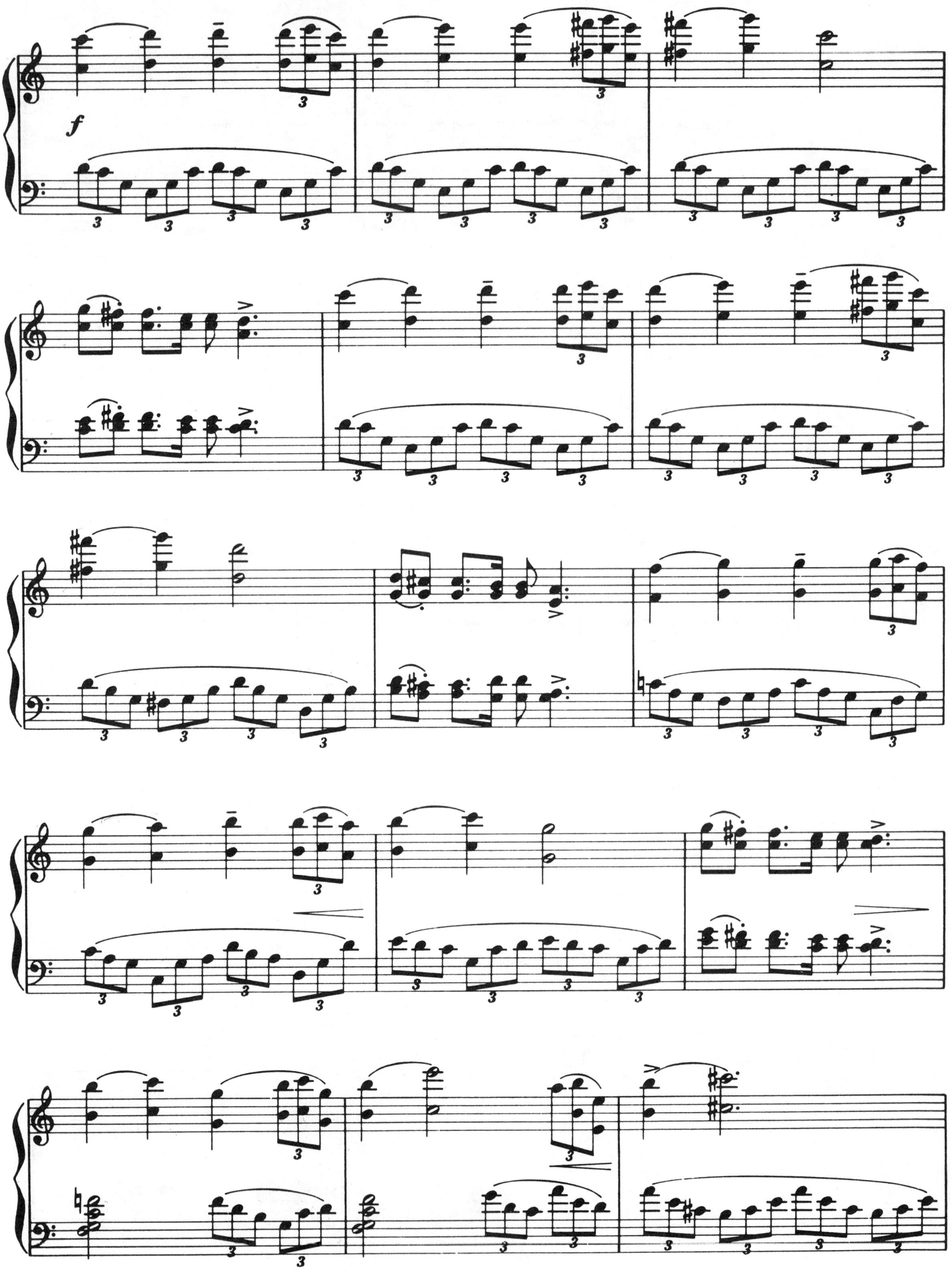
f

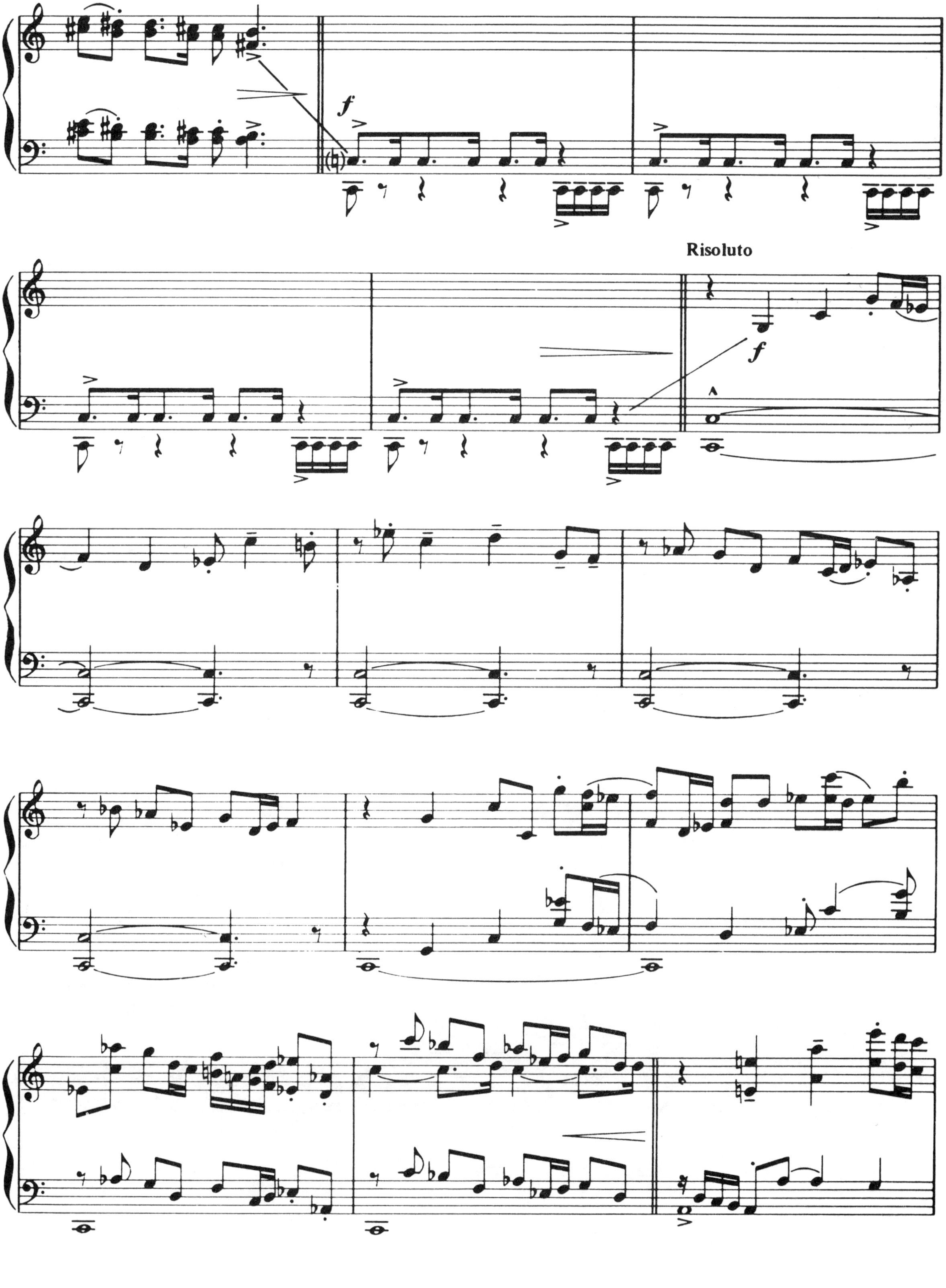
f
Risoluto
f

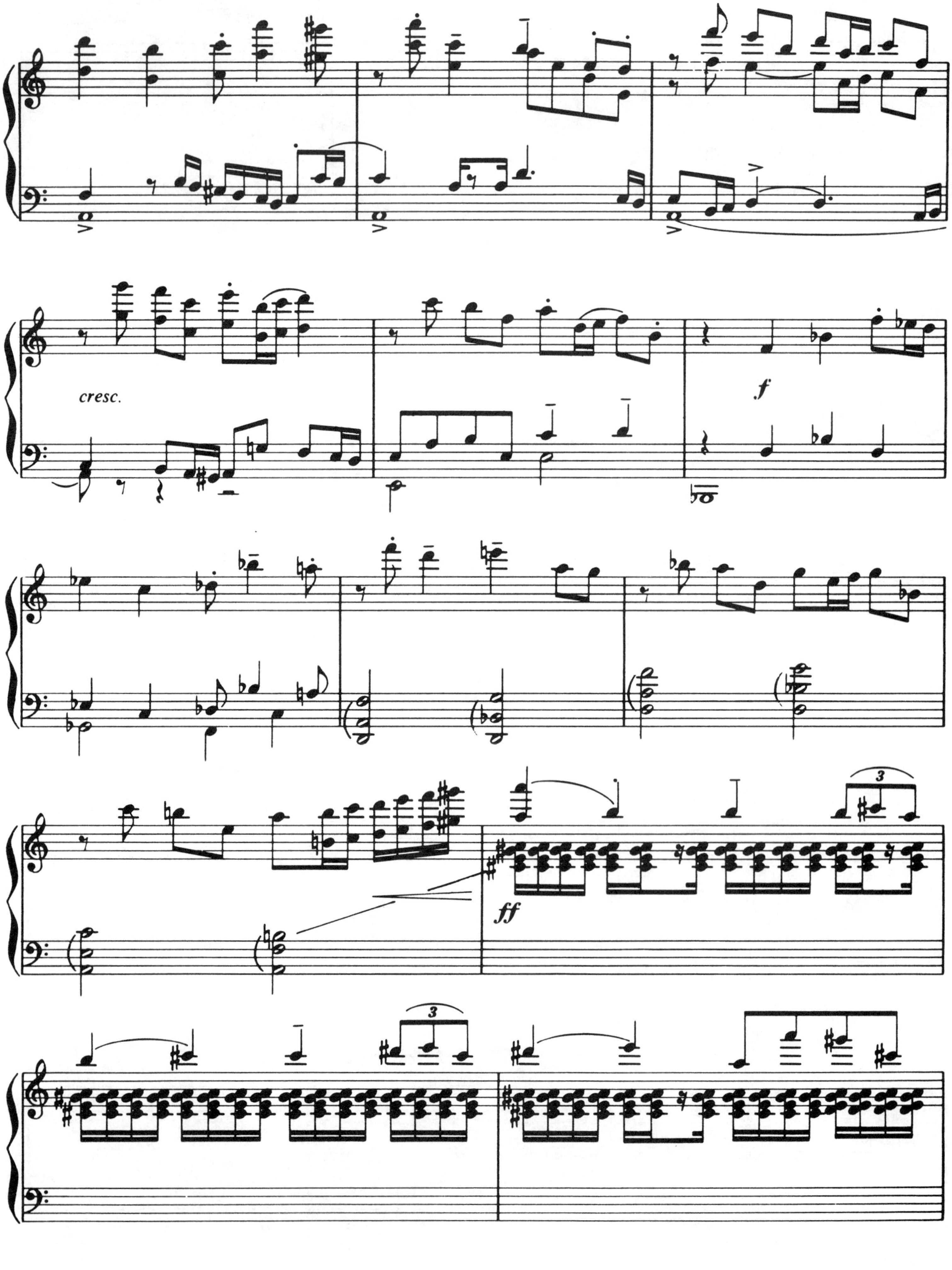
cresc.
f
3
ff
3

117

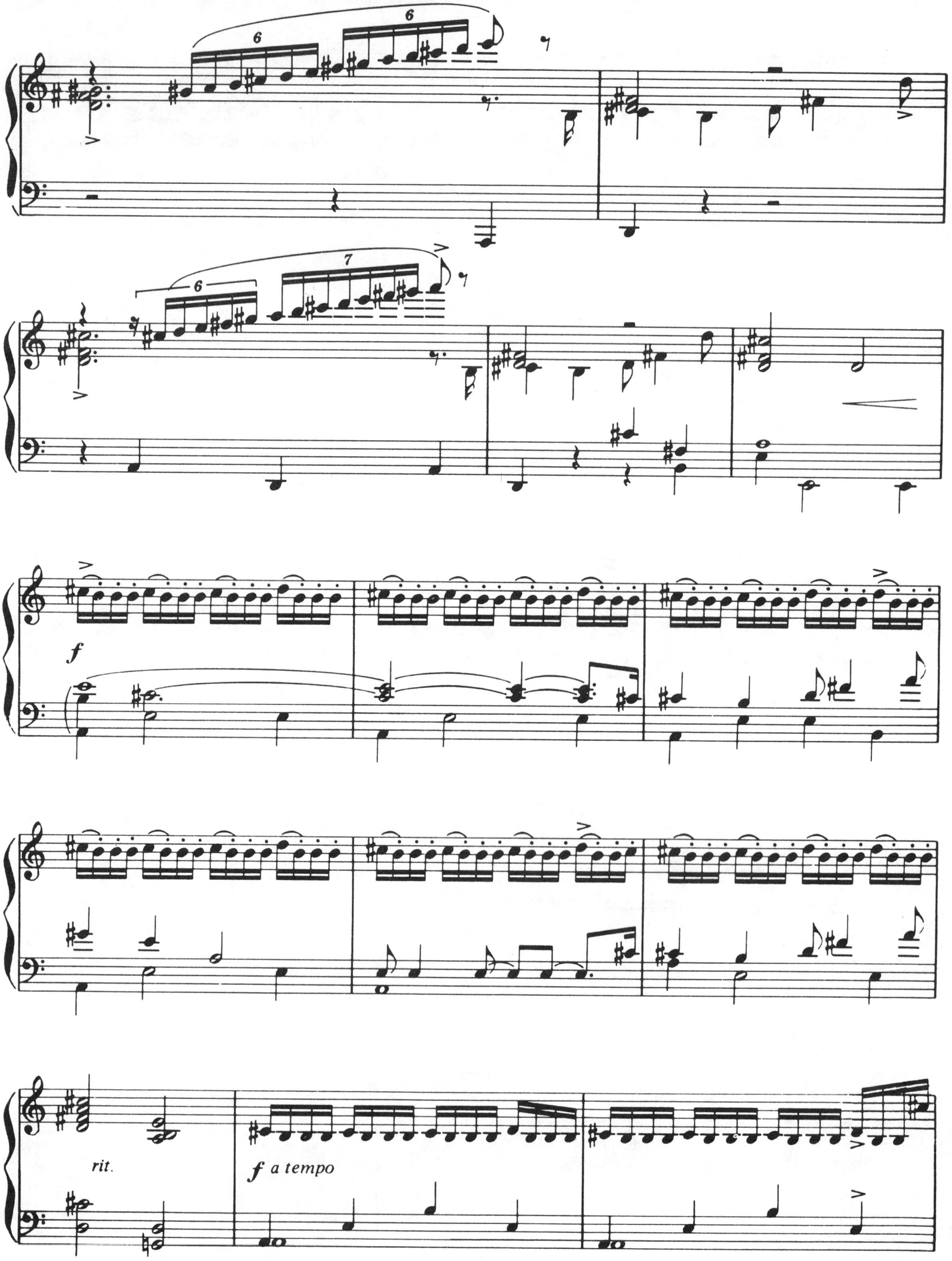
rit.
f a tempo

119

THEME FROM THE COWBOYS
A Warner Bros. Picture

By
JOHN WILLIAMS

Bright March

121

A HYMN TO NEW ENGLAND
(With Gratitude to David Mugar)

By
JOHN WILLIAMS

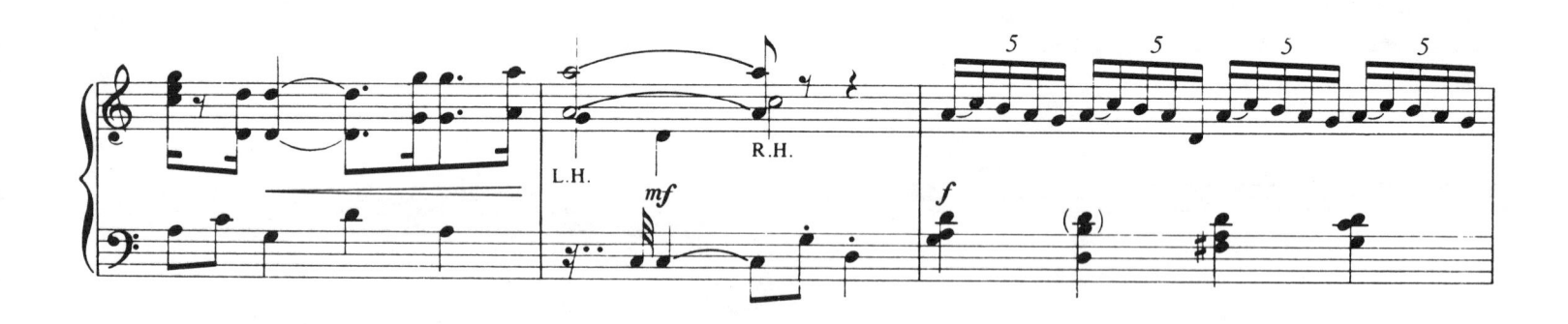

© 1989 MARJER PUBLISHING CO.
All rights administered by WARNER-TAMERLANE PUBLISHING CORP.
All Rights Reserved

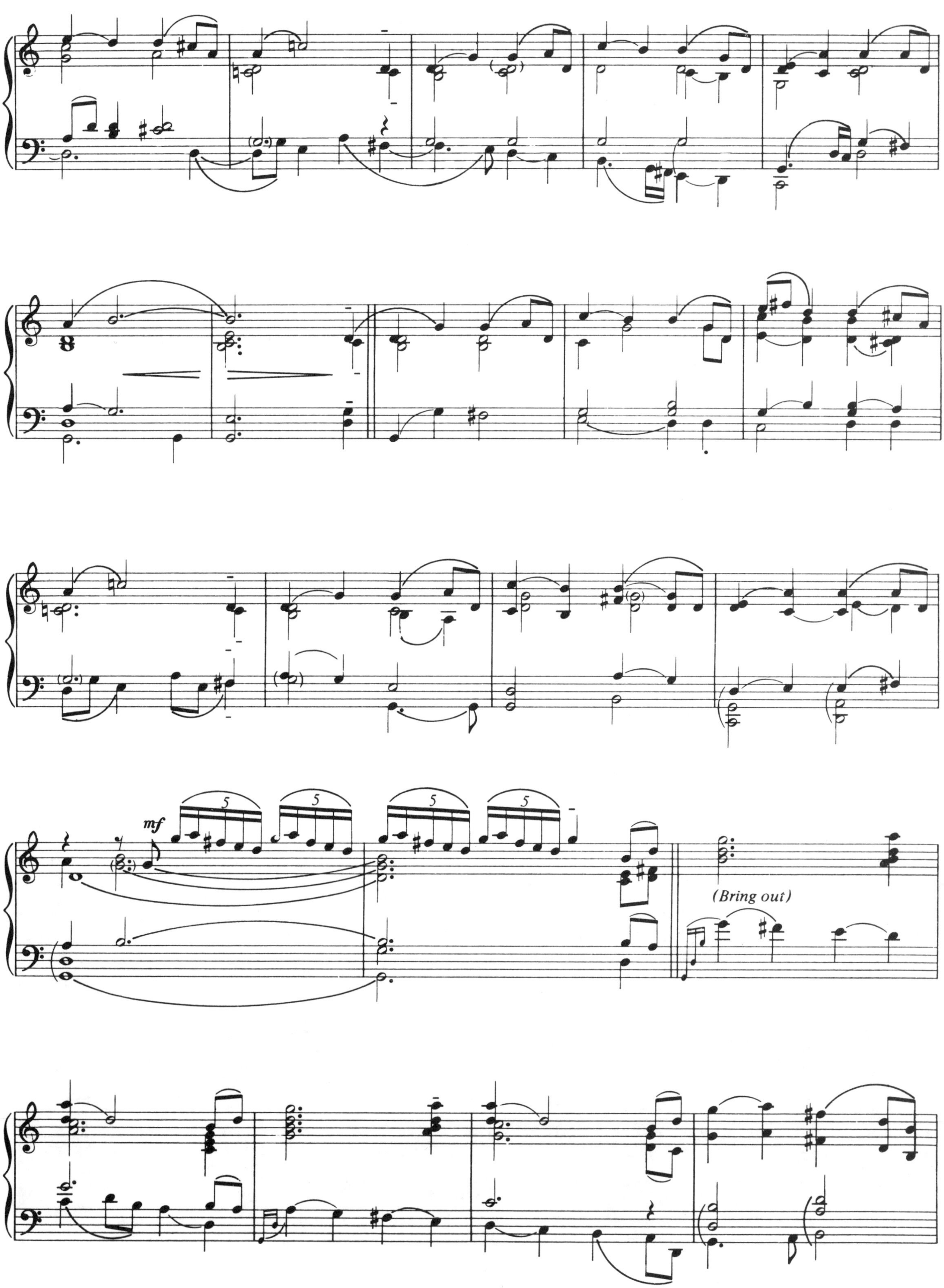
mf
5
5
5
5
(Bring out)

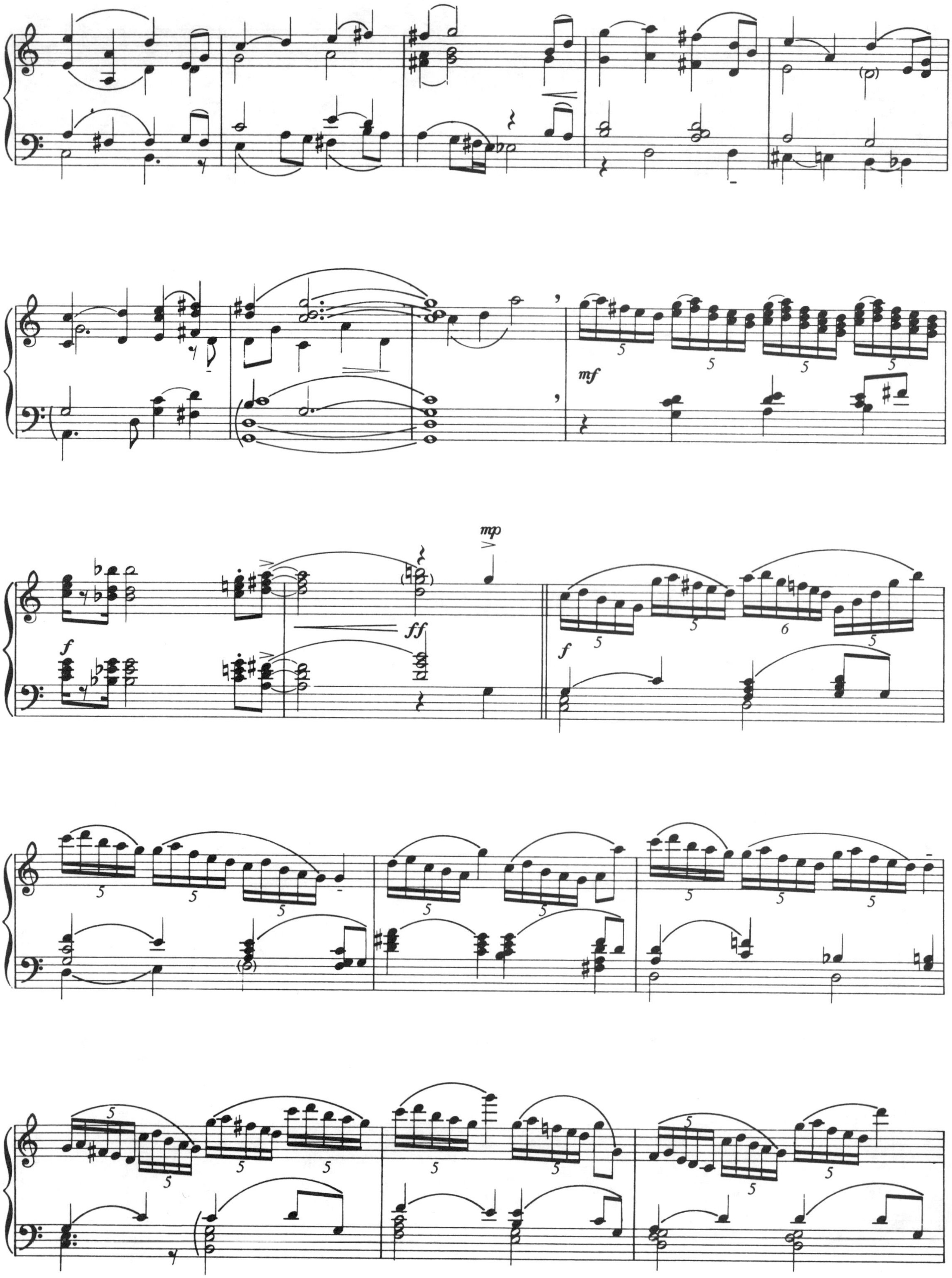
mf
mp
f
ff
f

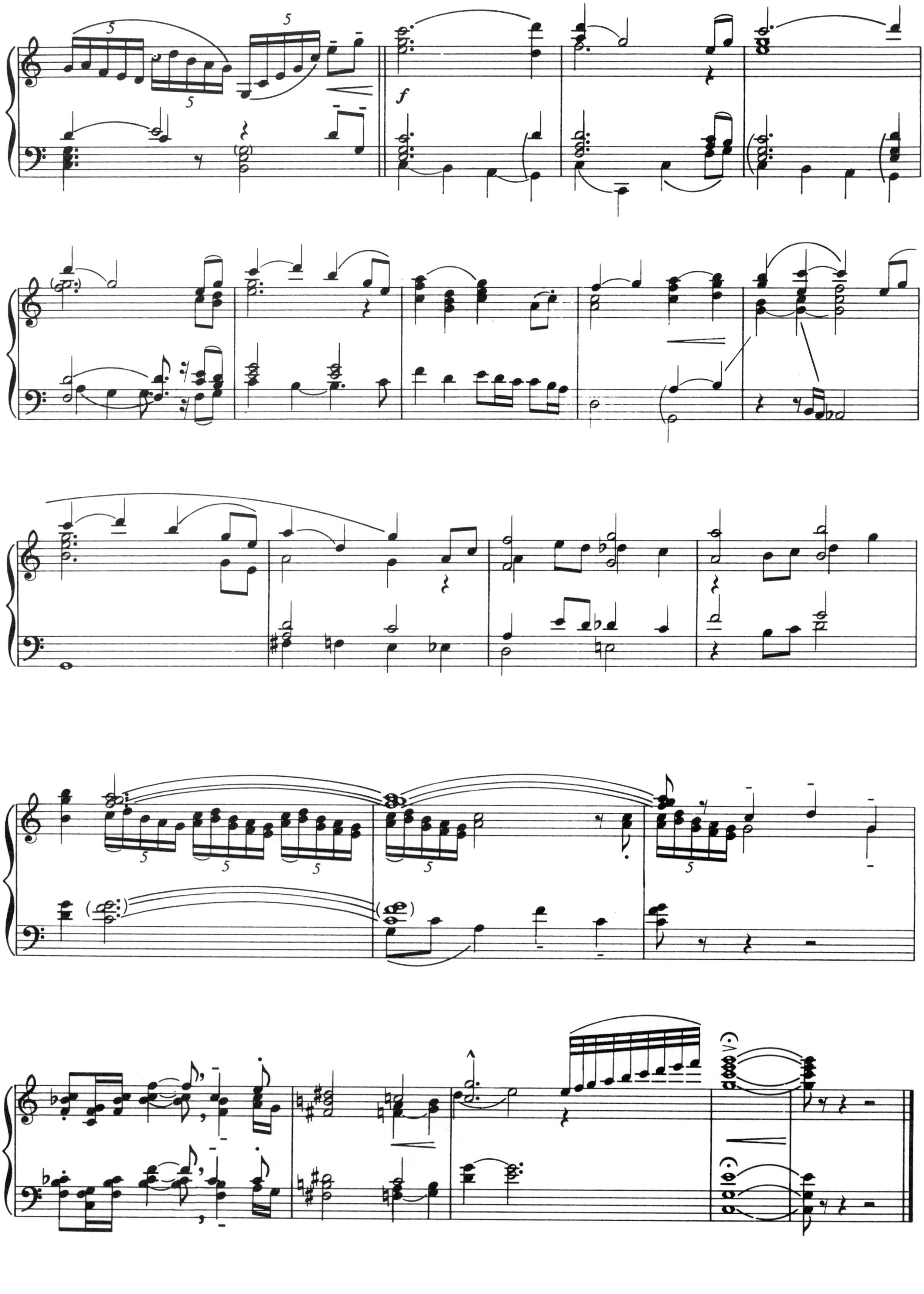

MAY THE FORCE BE WITH YOU

From "THE EMPIRE STRIKES BACK" A Lucasfilm Ltd. Production - A Twentieth Century-Fox Release

Music by
JOHN WILLIAMS

© 1980 WARNER-TAMERLANE PUBLISHING CORP. & BANTHA MUSIC
All rights administered by WARNER-TAMERLANE PUBLISHING CORP.
All Rights Reserved

Fm
Cm
Db
Db/C
Bbm7
Bbm7/Ab
Bbm/G
G7sus
G7
cresc.
dim. e rall.
Cm
Fm6
G+7
Cm
G7
Cm
a tempo
mf
F
G7
Cm
Cm/Bb
Ab
Cm/G
G7sus
G7
Cm

LIBERTY FANFARE

(Commissioned for the 100th Birthday of the Statue of Liberty July 3, 1986)

By
JOHN WILLIAMS

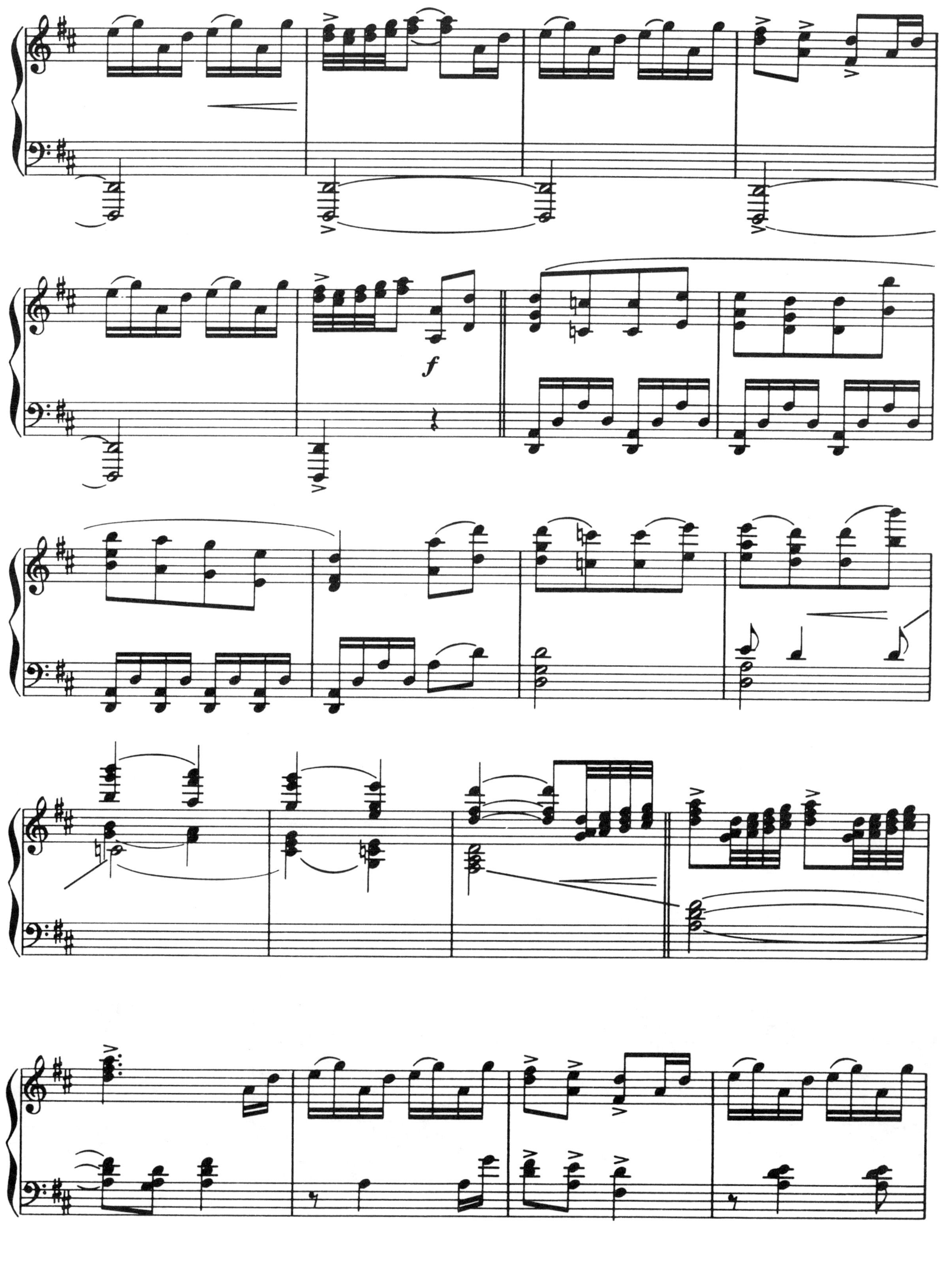
f

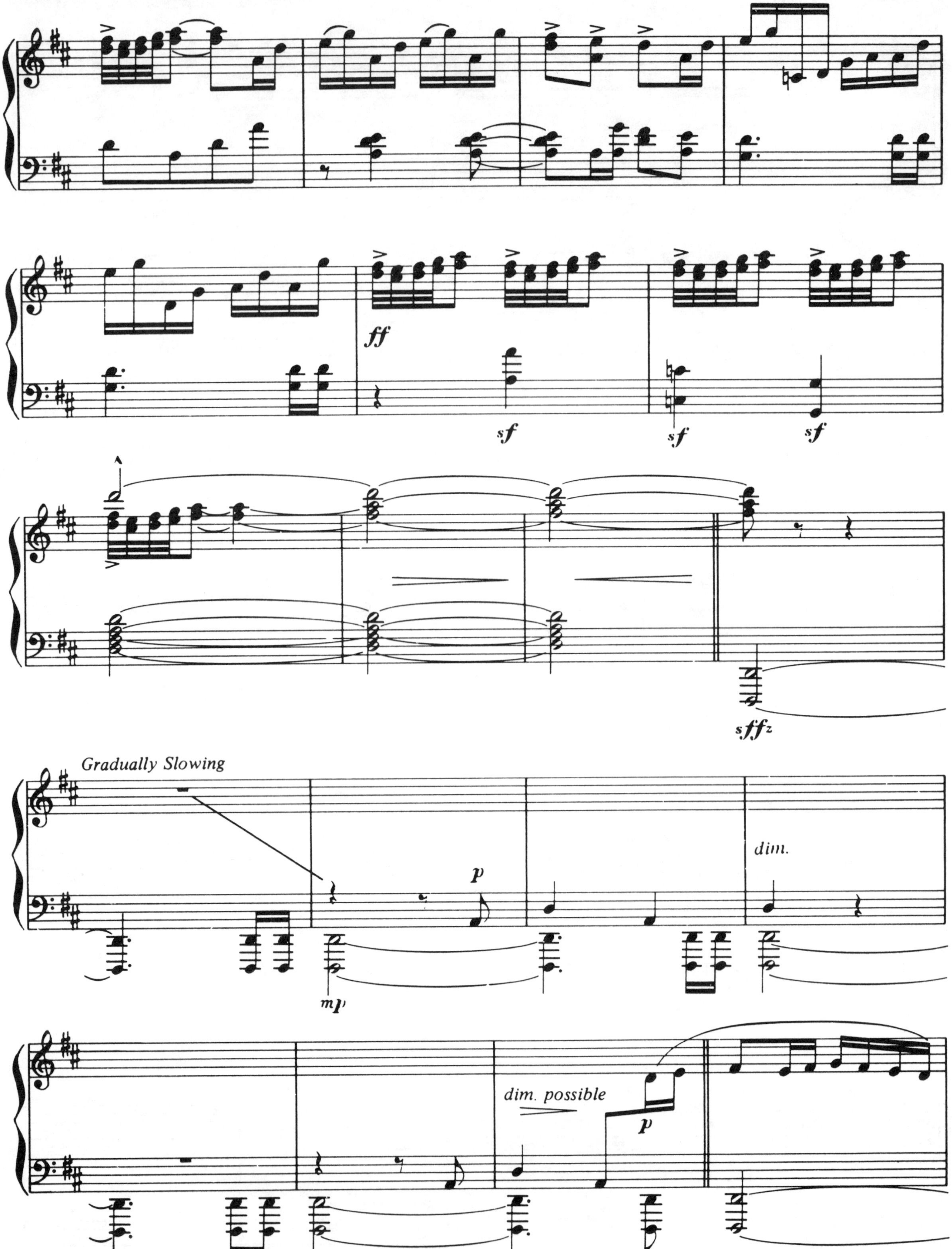
ff
sf
sf
sf
sffz
Gradually Slowing
p
mp
dim.
dim. possible
p

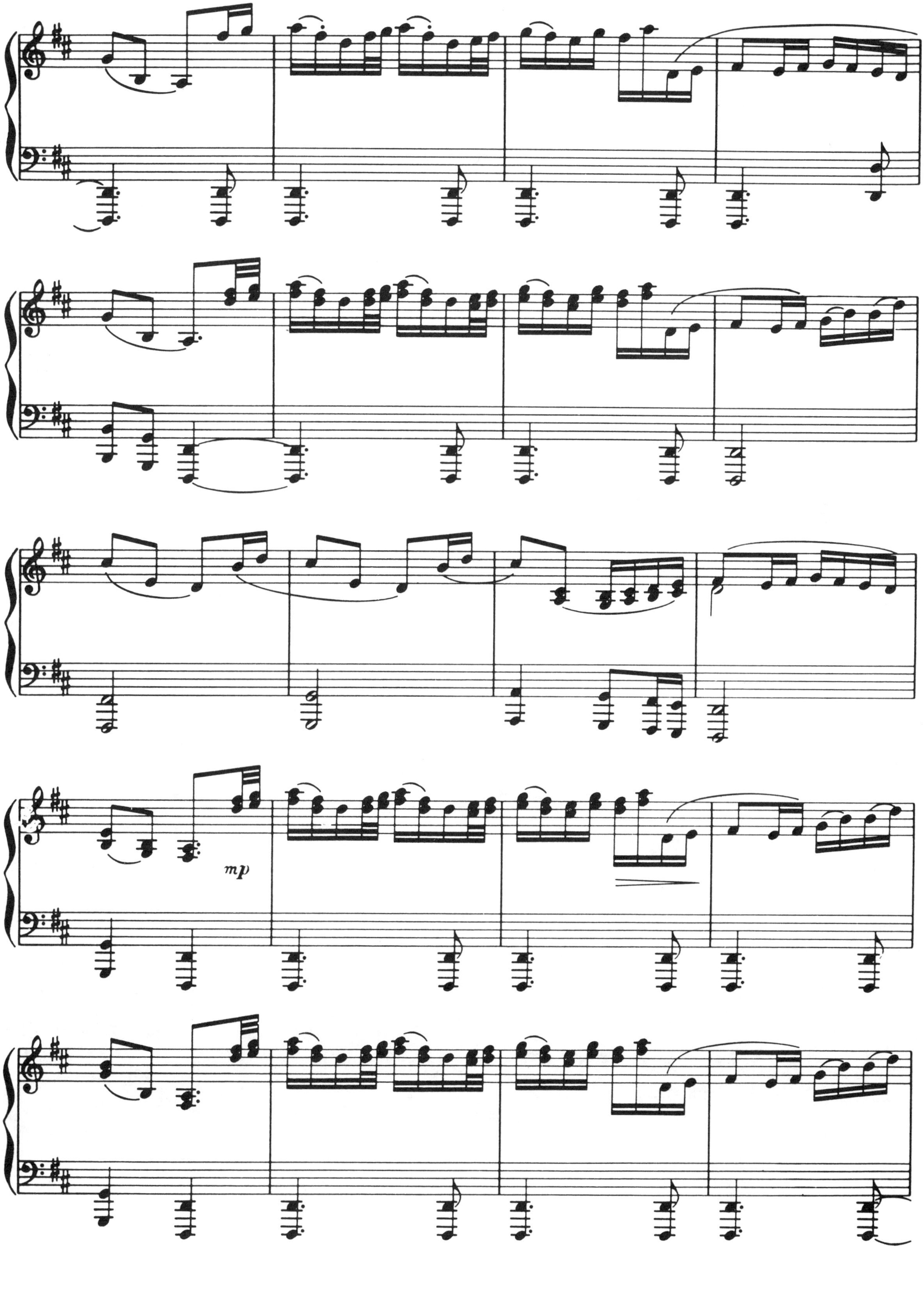
mp

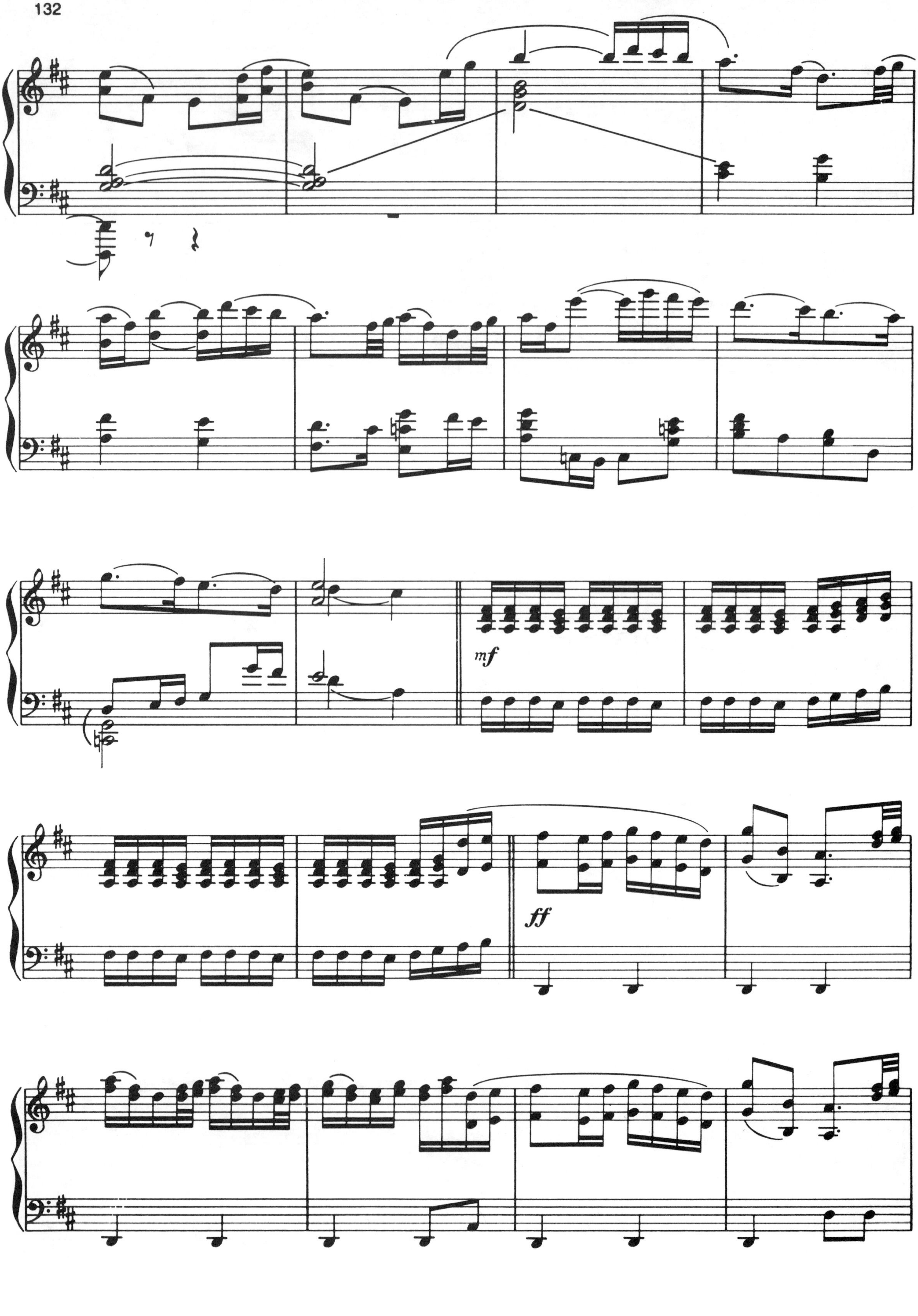
mf
ff

133

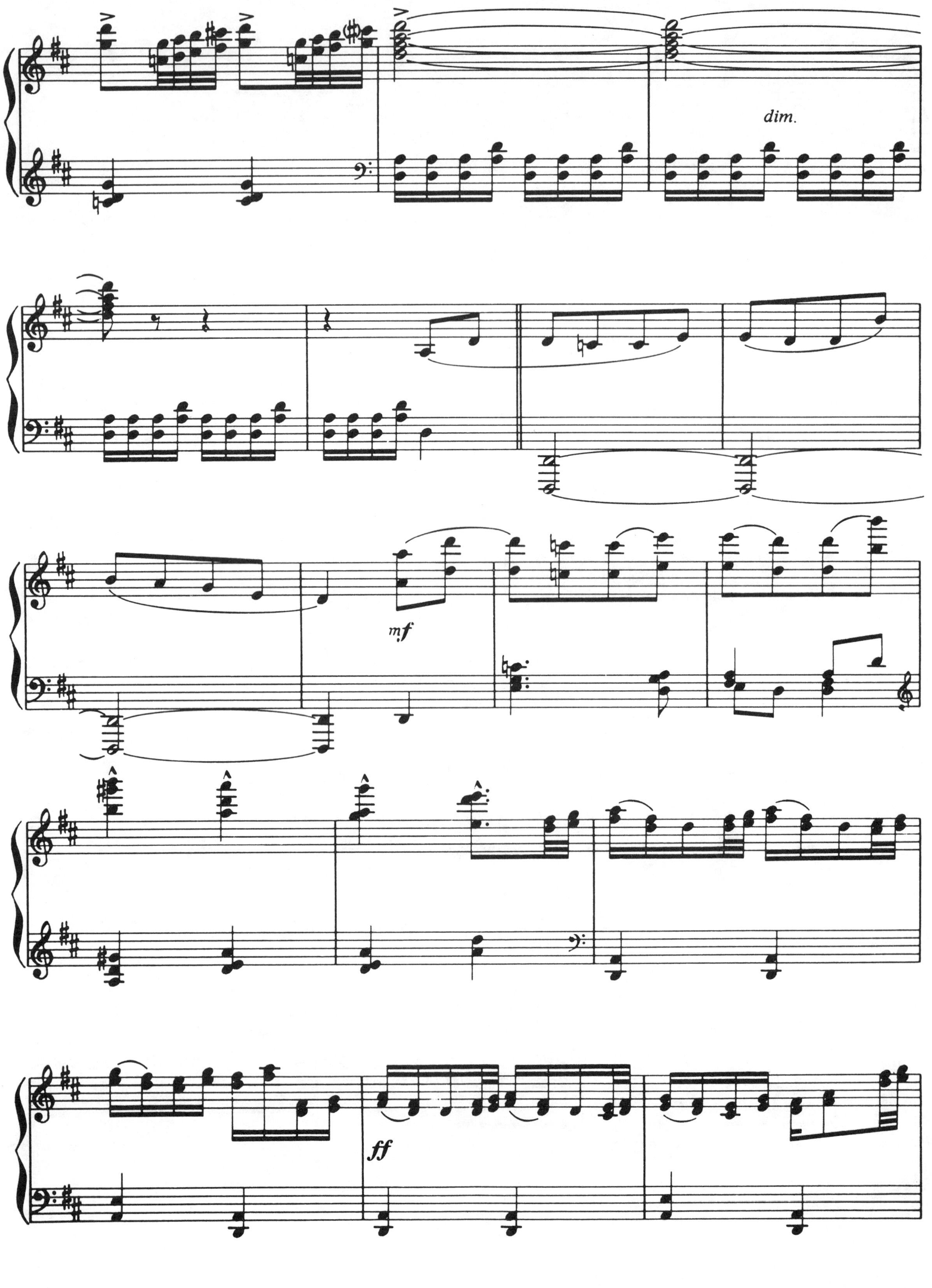
dim.
mf
ff

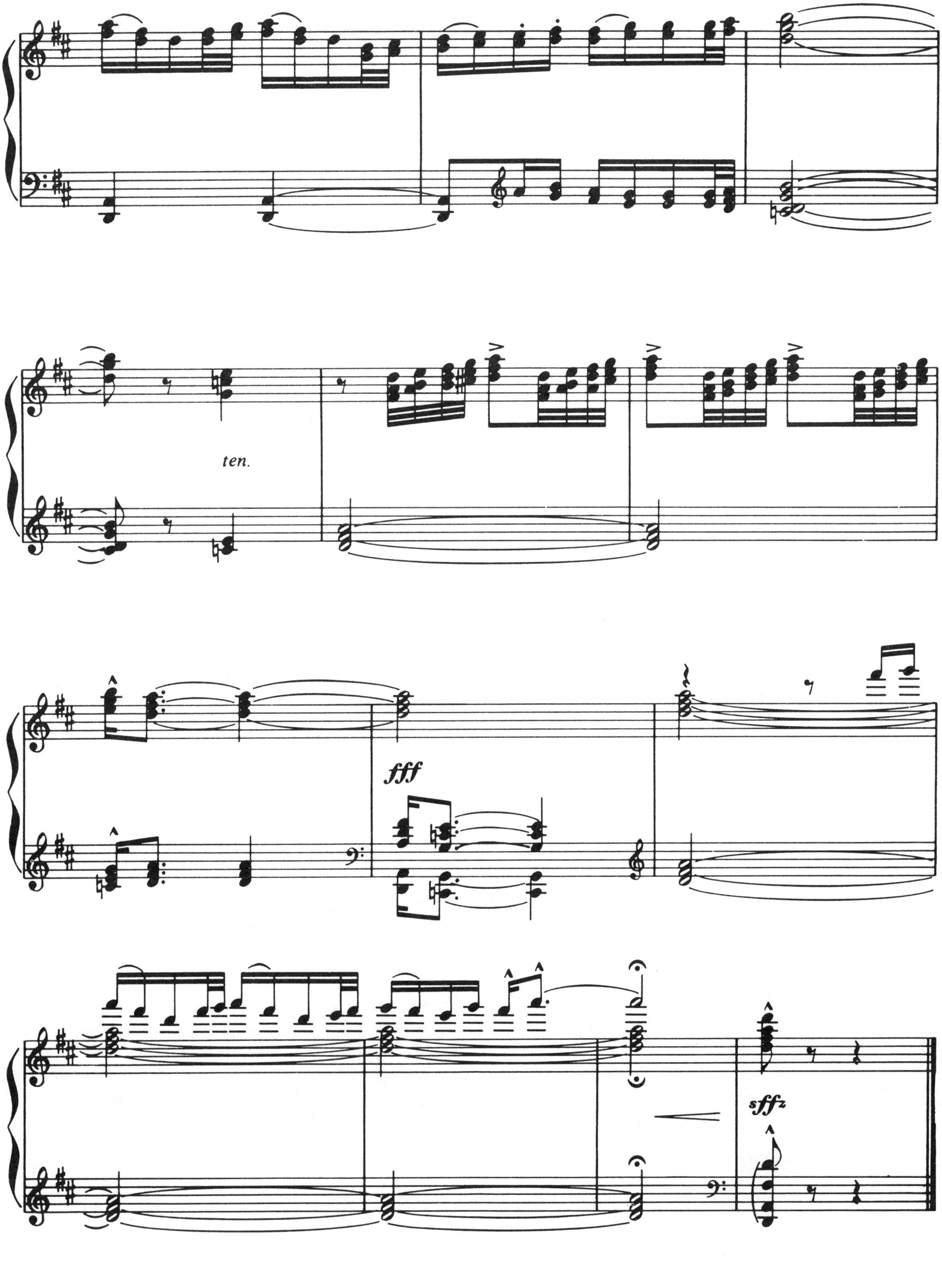
ten.
fff
sffz

EXSULTATE JUSTI

(From The Motion Picture "EMPIRE OF THE SUN")

Words and Music by
JOHN WILLIAMS

© 1987, 1988 WARNER-TAMERLANE PUBLISHING CORP. (BMI)
All Rights Reserved

ta - te ju - sti in Do - mi - no Ex - sul - ta - te in Do - mi -
no. Ex - sul - ta - te ju - sti in Do - mi - no. Rec - tos
de - cet la - da - ti - o. Al - le - lu - ia, Al - le - lu - ia,

a. Al - le - lu - ia, Al - le - lu - ia - a. Sal - va - tor
Do - mi-nus Sal - va - tor mun - di. Qui tol - lis Pec - ca - ta
mu - n - di. Sal - va - tor Do - mi - nus. Sal - va - tor

mun - di. Qui tol - lis Pec - ca - ta mu - n - mun - n - di.

Tutti **f**
Al - le - lu - ia, Al - le - lu - ia - a.

Boys choir
Ex - sul - ta - te Ju - sti in Do - mi - no Rec - tos
Al - le - lu - ia, Al - le - lu - ia, - a. Rec - tos

De - cet la - da - ti - o.

To Coda ⊕

Lau - da - mus te. Lau - da - mus. Lau - da - mus te.

Lauda-mus. Lauda-mus te. Lauda-mus, Lauda-mus Lauda-mus.

Can-tate e— i. Can-ticum no-vum.

Can-
Can-tate e— i.— Can-
Can-tate e— i.— Can-

ta - te e - i. Bene Psallite e-
ti - cum no - vum. Bene psal-
ta - te e - i. Canticum

i, in vociferatio-
li - te - i in vo - ci - te ra - ti-
no - vum can - ti - cum no

ne. Lau-
o - ne. Lauda - mus te. Lauda - mus Lau-
vum.

143

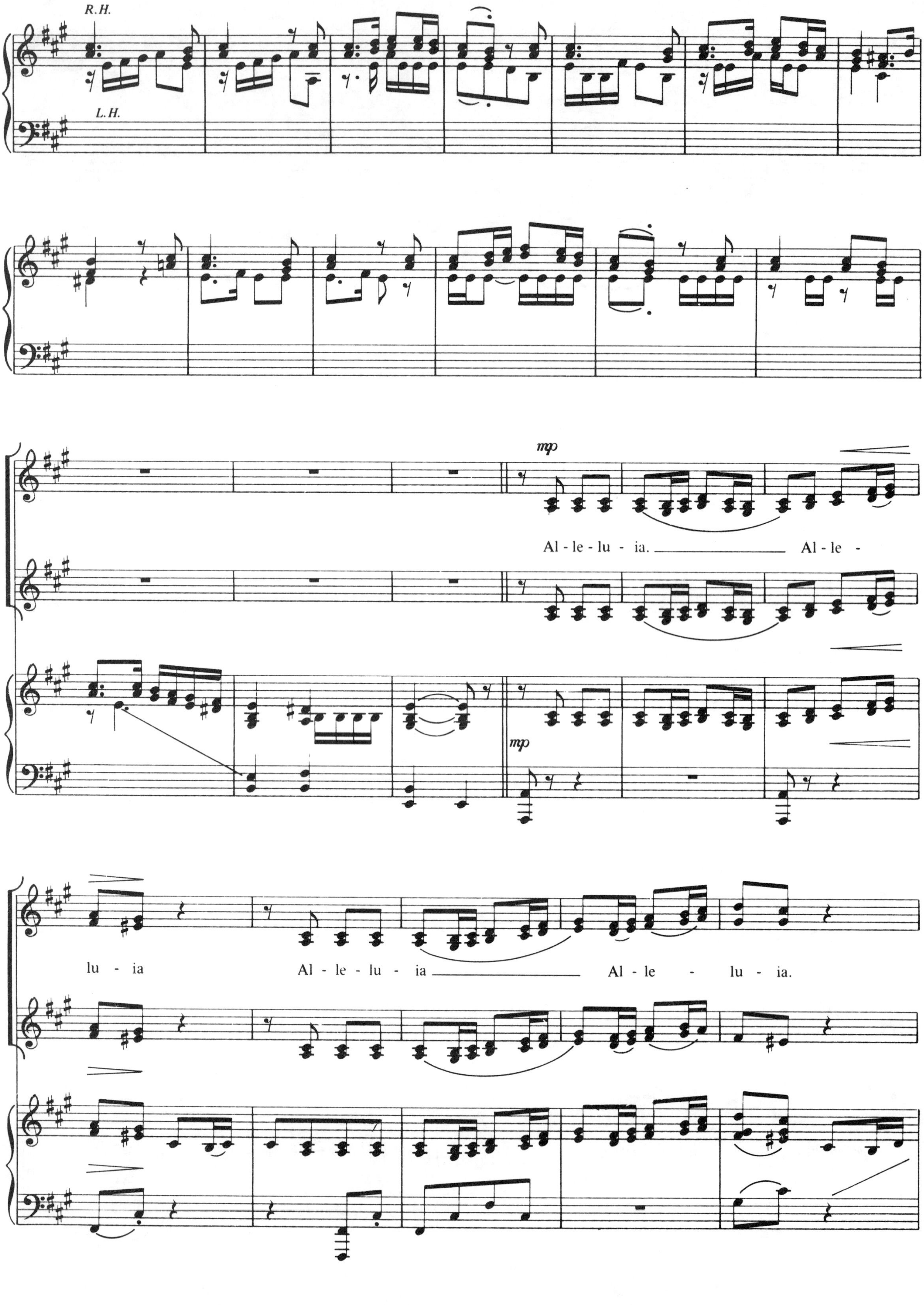
R.H.
L.H.
mp
Al - le - lu - ia. Al - le -
mp
lu - ia
Al - le - lu - ia
Al - le - lu - ia.

145

ia. Al - le lu - ia.
p
Lau - da - mus
p
D.S. al Coda
te. Lau - da - mus Lau - da - mus te. Lau - da - mus

Coda
Ex - sul - ta te___ ju - sti in_ Do-mi-no Rec - tos___
De Cet-la - da - ti - o.___ Ex - sul - ta - te___
rall. e cresc.
ju - sti in_ Do - mi-no. Ex - sul - ta - te in Do - min - no.

TOYPLANES, HOME AND HEARTH

(From the Motion Picture "EMPIRE OF THE SUN")

By
JOHN WILLIAMS

149

Tenderly, with movement

151

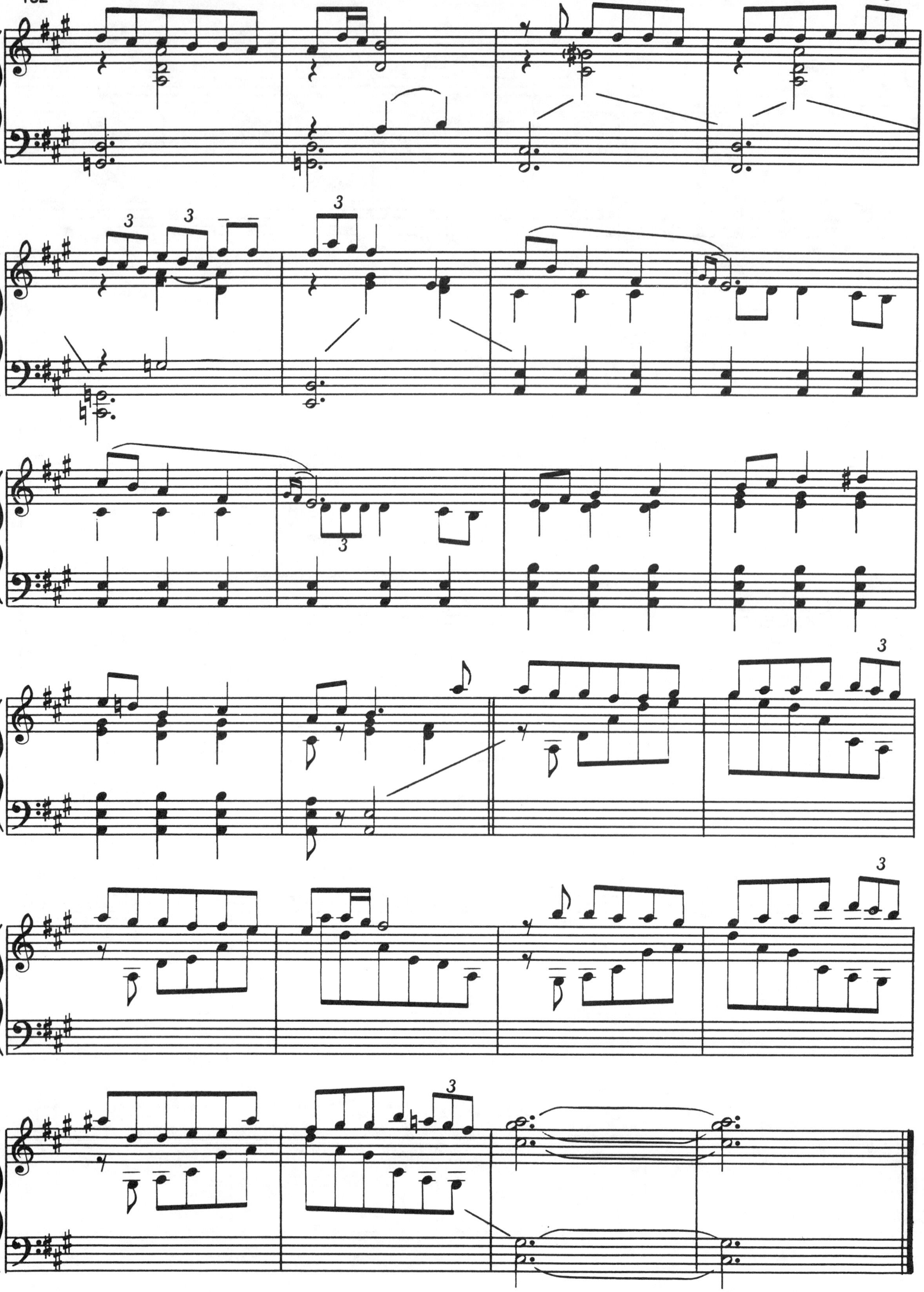

WINTER GAMES FANFARE

(Written especially for the 1989 World Alpine Ski Championship, Vail, Colorado)

By JOHN WILLIAMS

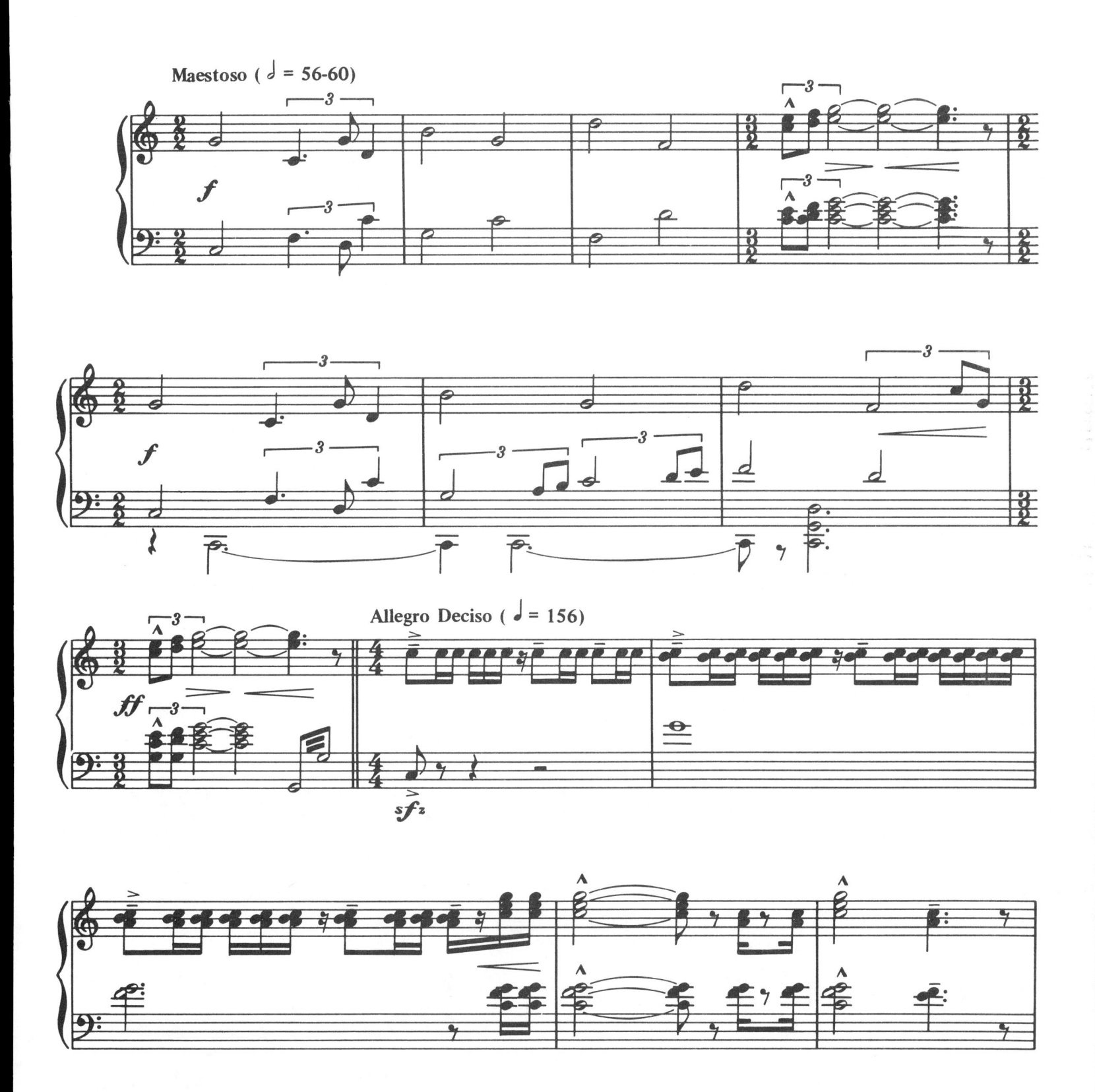

© 1989 MARJER PUBLISHING CO.
All rights administered by WARNER-TAMERLANE PUBLISHING CORP.
All Rights Reserved

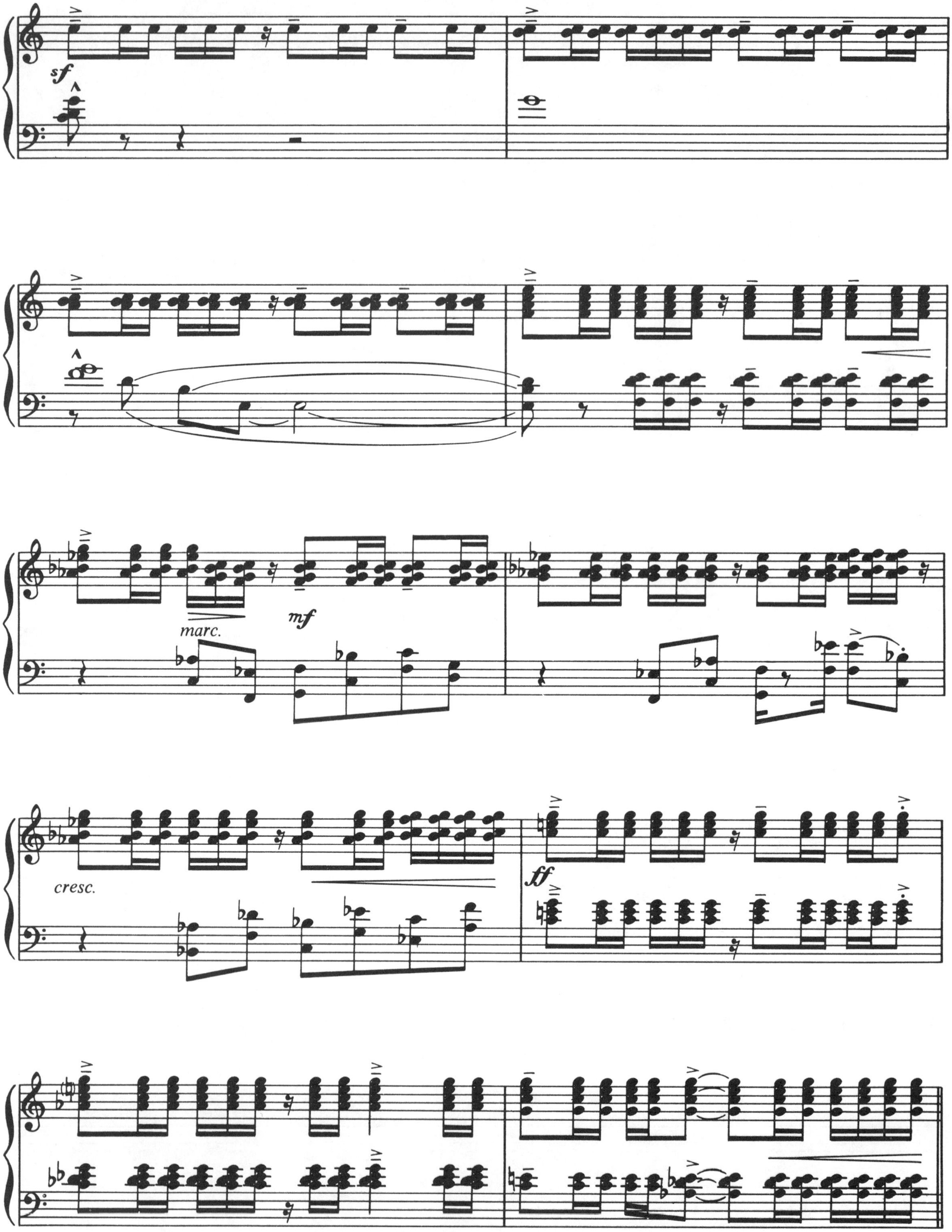
sf
marc.
mf
cresc.
ff

155

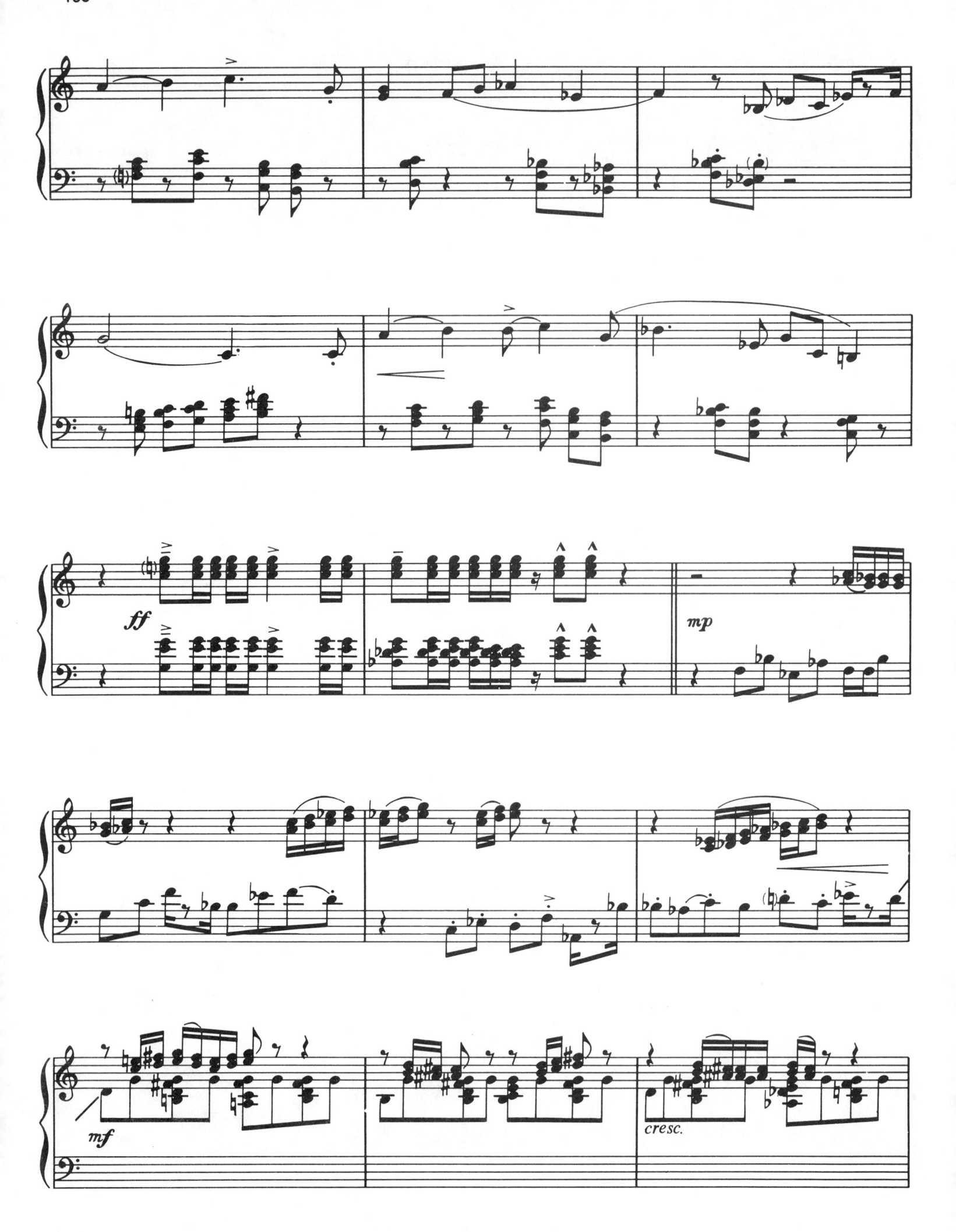
ff
mp
mf
cresc.

157

158

Maestoso (𝅗𝅥 = 56)
ff
sffz
rall. e cresc. molto
Presto
marcato
Maestoso
cresc.
poco

THEME FROM THE ACCIDENTAL TOURIST

By
JOHN WILLIAMS

161

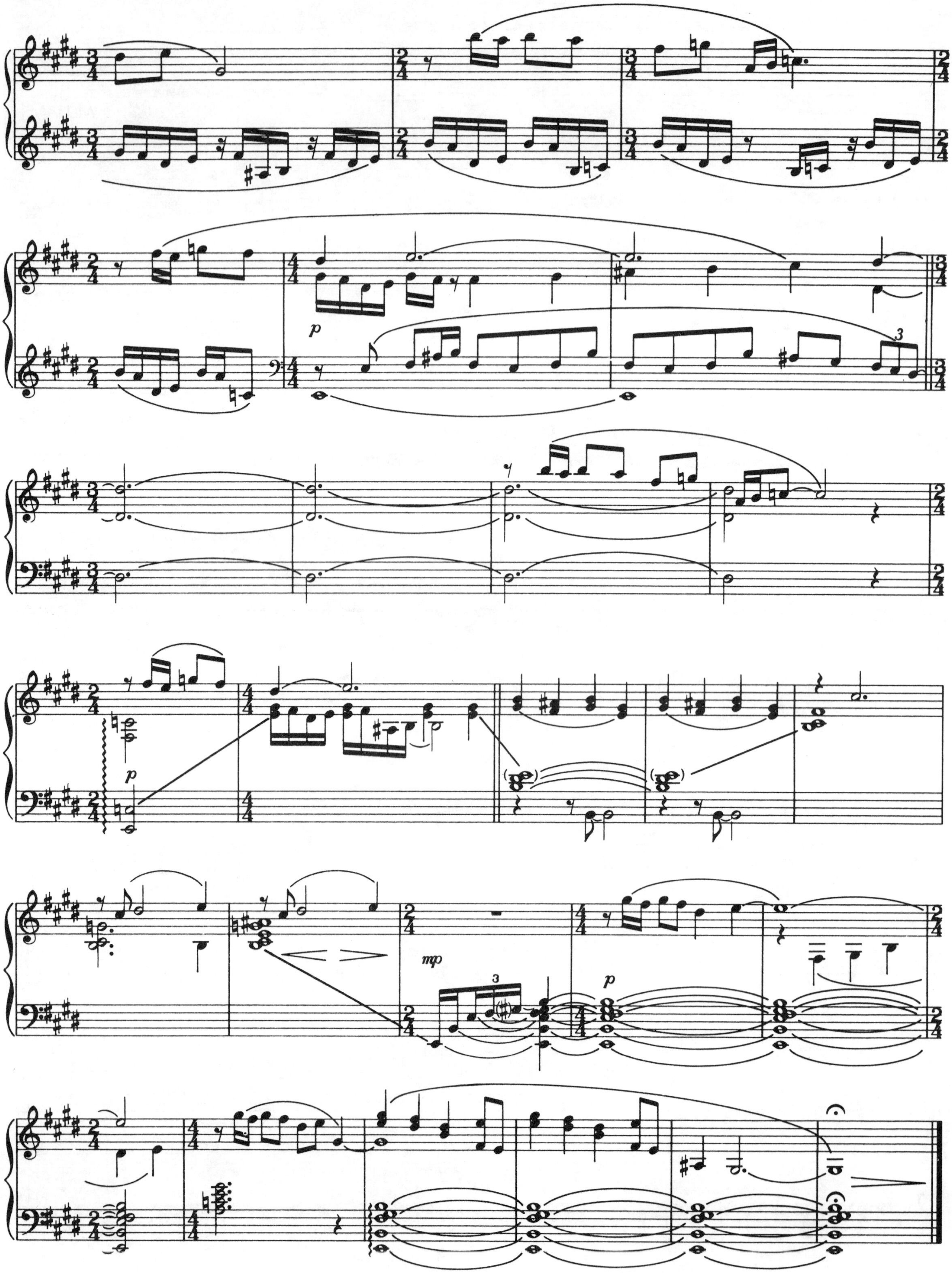

Somewhere in My Memory

From the Twentieth Century-Fox Feature Film "HOME ALONE"

Words by
LESLIE BRICUSSE

Music by
JOHN WILLIAMS

Gently and with simplicity

smoothly
mp

Can - dles in the win - dow, shad - ows paint - ing the ceil - ing,

© 1990 FOX FILM MUSIC CORPORATION/JOHN HUGHES SONGS (BMI)
All rights for JOHN HUGHES SONGS controlled and administered by SCREEN GEMS-EMI MUSIC INC.
All Rights Reserved

gazing at the fire glow, feeling that "gin-ger-bread" feel - ing. Pre-cious mo - ments, spe-cial peo - ple, hap-py fac - es I can see. Some-where in my mem - 'ry, Christ-mas joys all a - round me, living in my mem-'ry, all of the mu-sic, all of the mag-ic, all of the fam-'ly home here with me.

REMEMBERING CAROLYN
(A Theme from "PRESUMED INNOCENT")

Music by
JOHN WILLIAMS

© 1990 WARNER-TAMERLANE PUBLISHING CORP.
All Rights Reserved

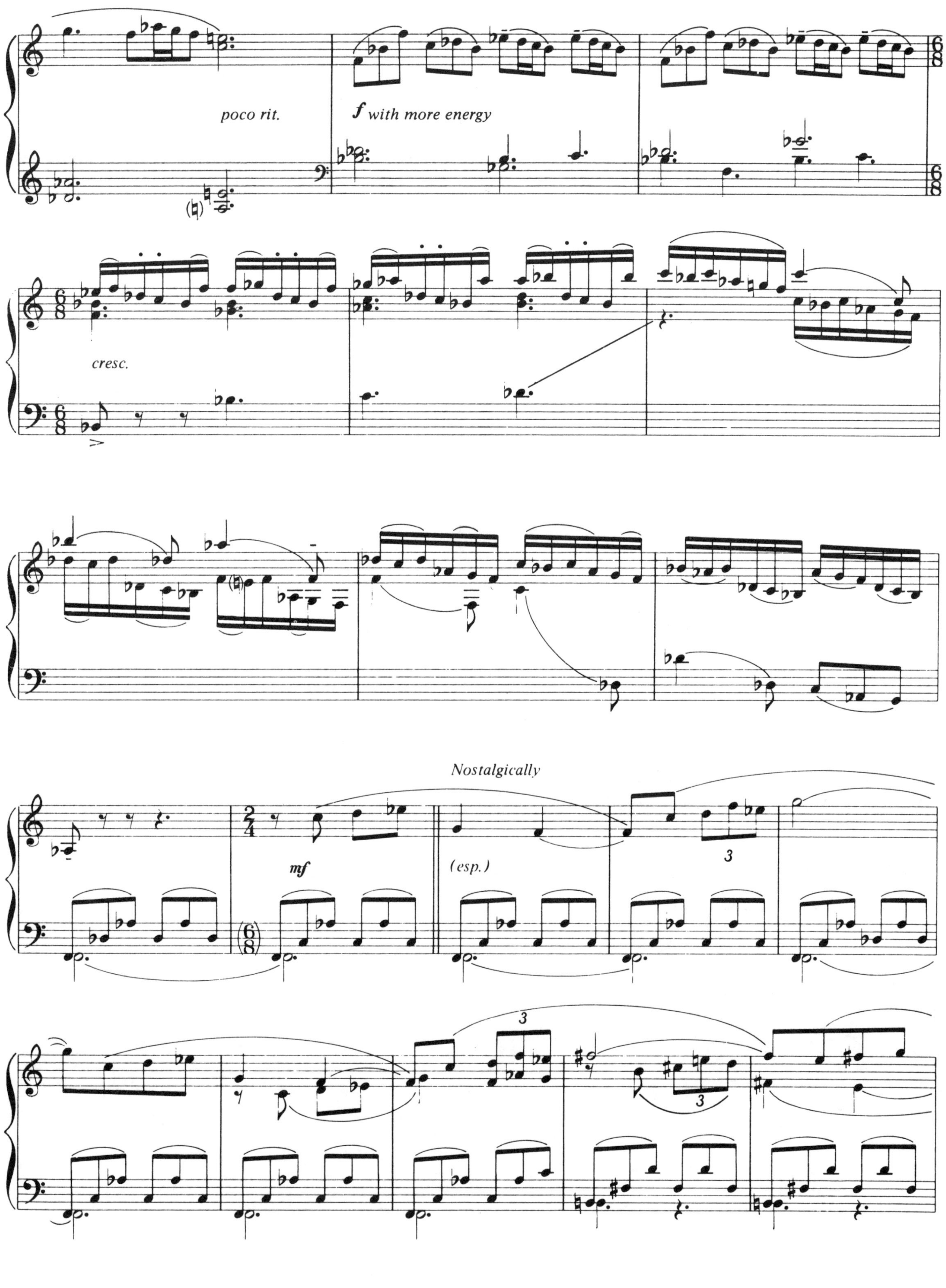
poco rit.
f with more energy
cresc.
Nostalgically
mf
(esp.)

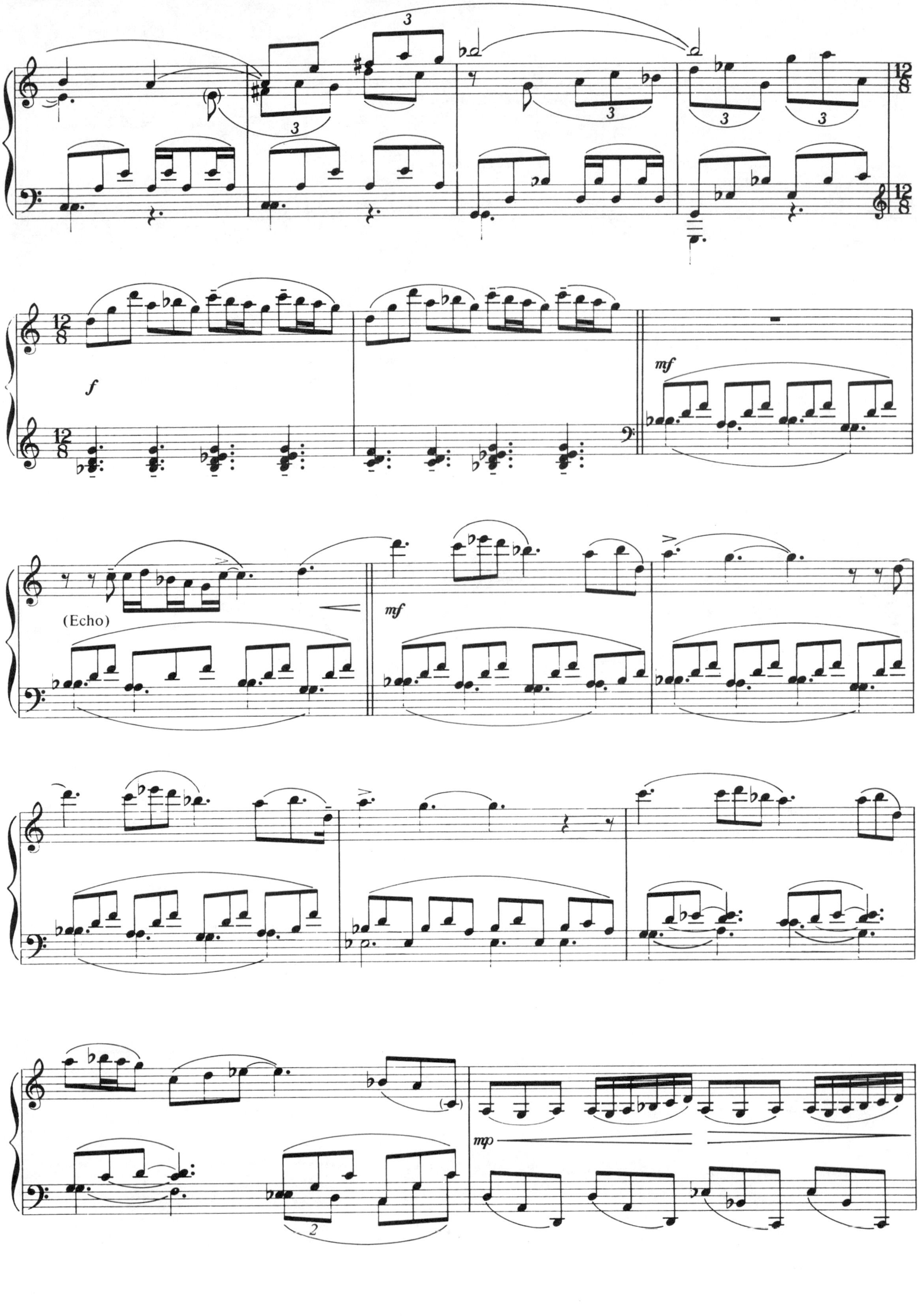
f
mf
(Echo)
mf
mp

p subito
mf
cresc. molto
f
mf
(Echo)
L.H.
Rubato (cantabile)
rall.
(mf)
(riten)
molto rit.
(Pedal down)

THE OLYMPIC SPIRIT

By
JOHN WILLIAMS

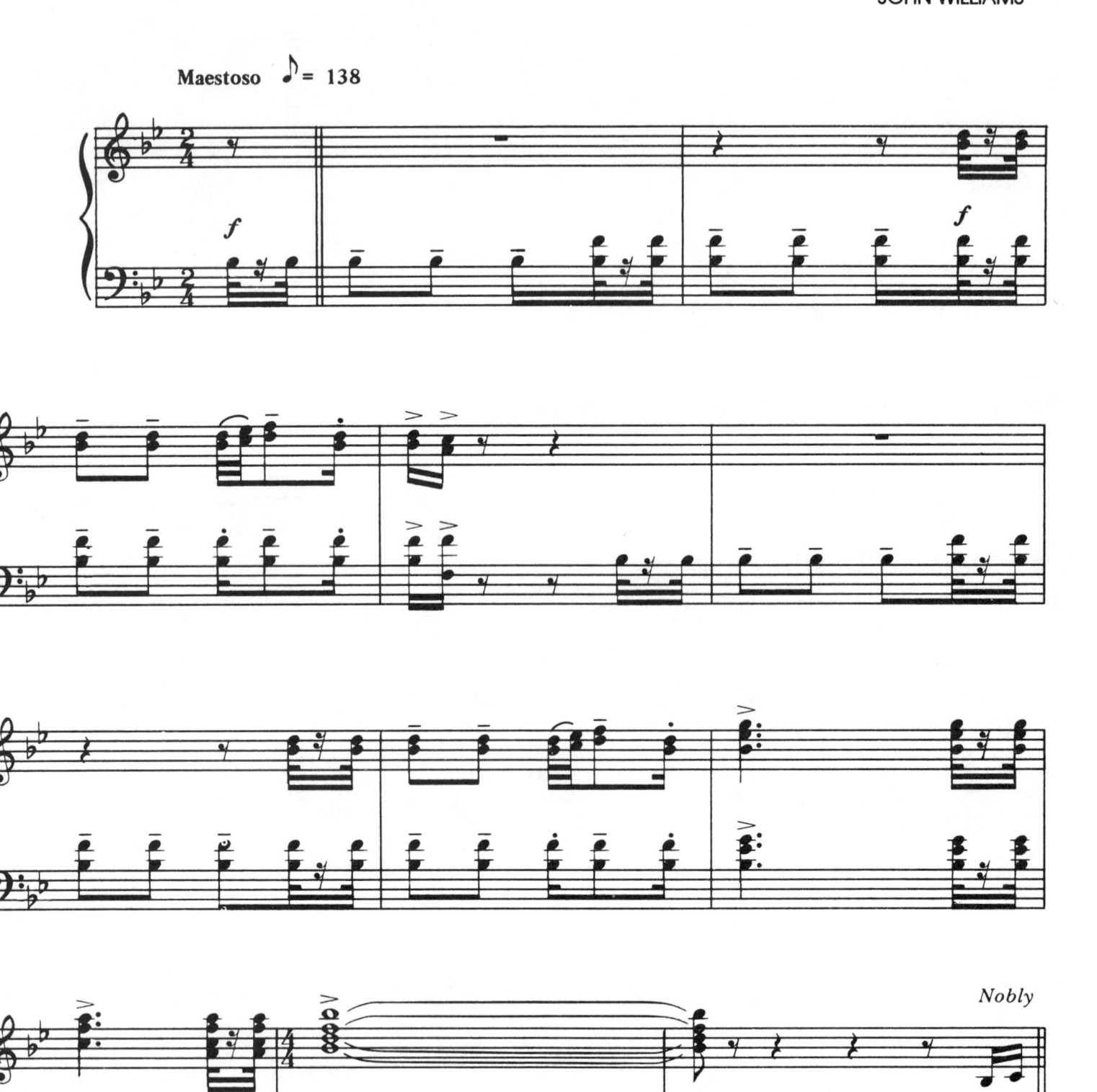

171

172

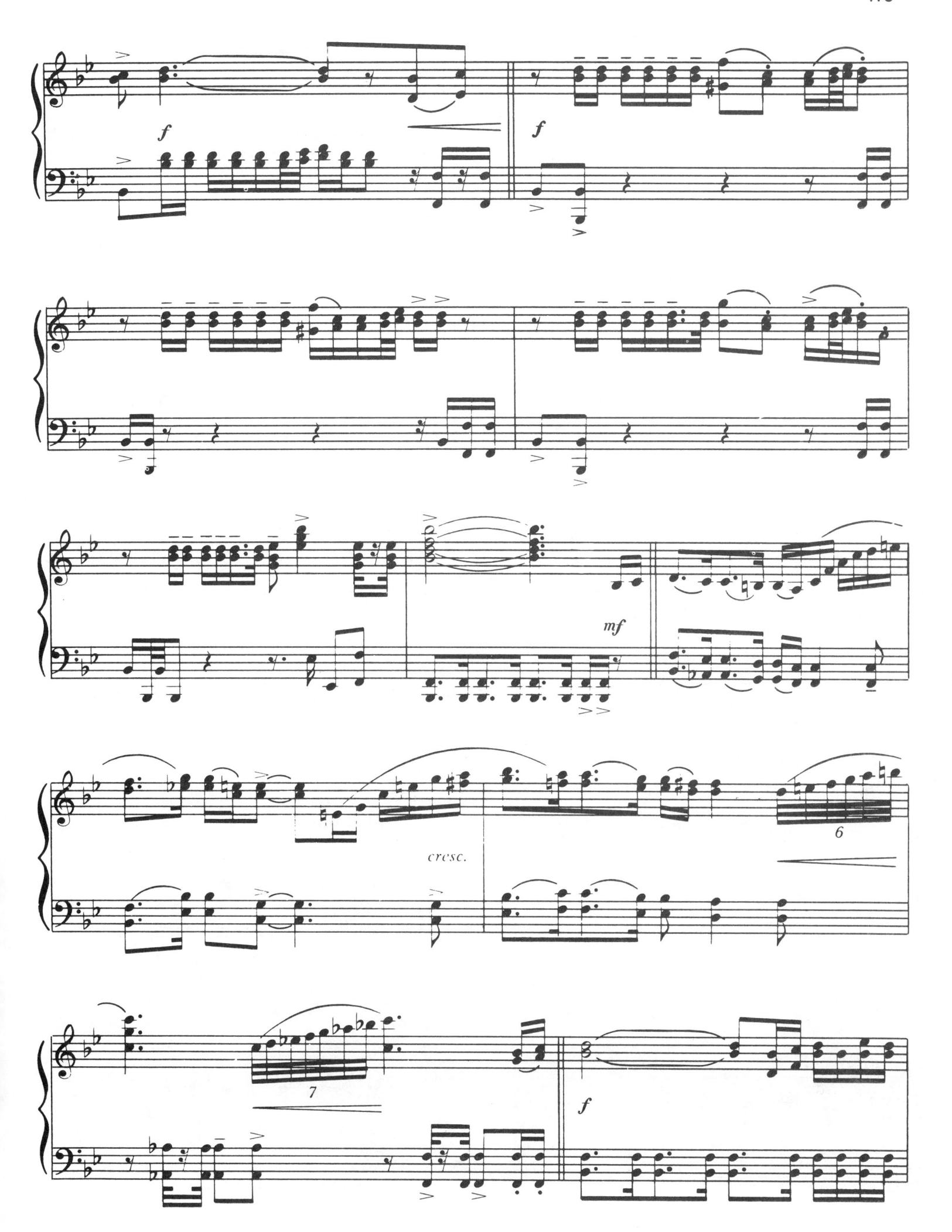
f
f
mf
cresc.
6
7
f

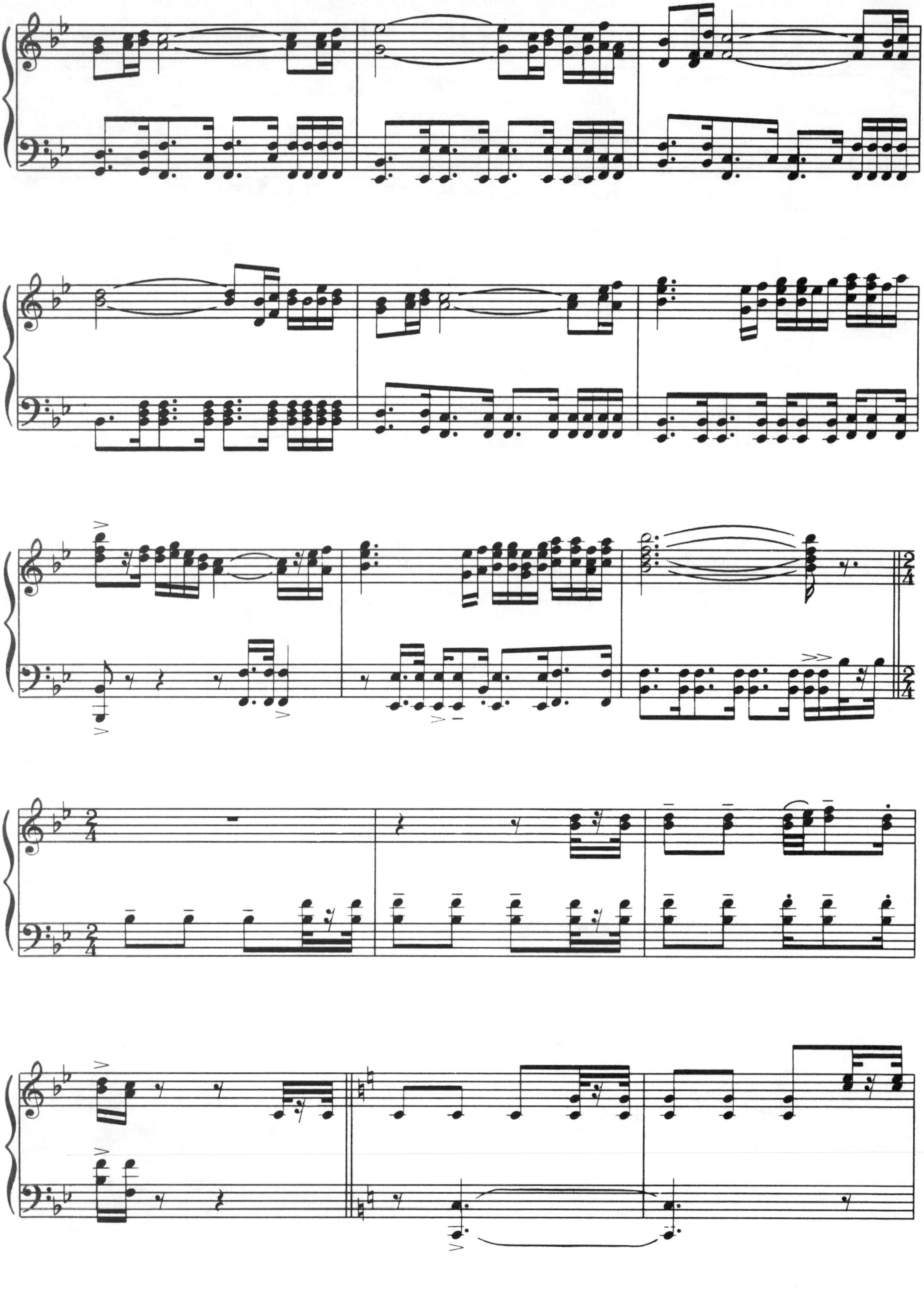

175

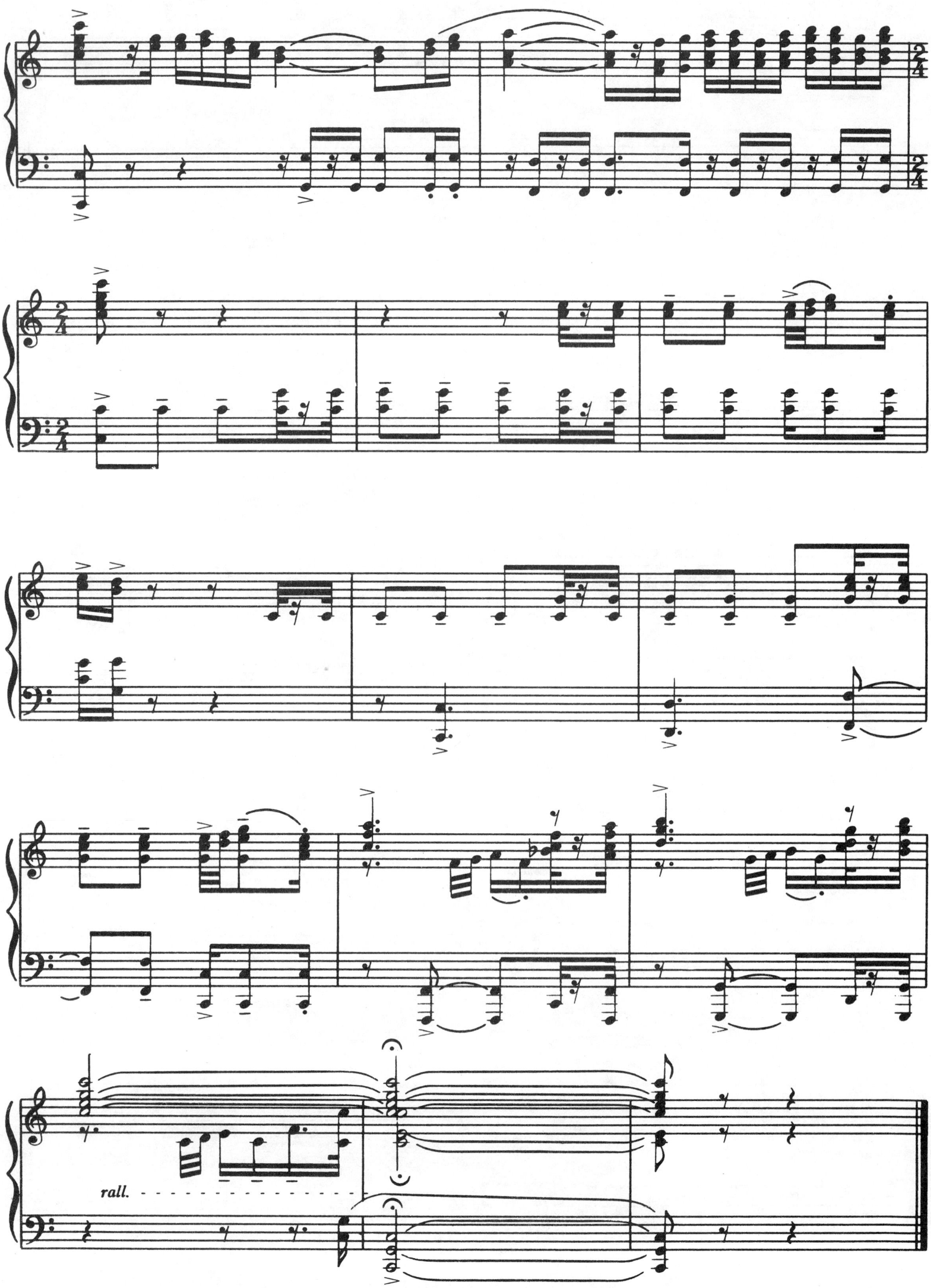
rall.